PERSPECTIVES ON ORGANIZATIONS

The School as a Social Organization

by

Ronald G. Corwin and Roy A. Edelfelt

Edited by

Theodore E. Andrews and Brenda L. Bryant

American Association of Colleges
for Teacher Education
and
Association of Teacher Educators
Washington, D.C.

ACKNOWLEDGMENTS

The materials were prepared under Contract #300-75-0100 to the University of Nebraska from the United States Office of Education. The opinions expressed herein should not necessarily be construed as representing the opinions of the United States Office of Educati◄

Cover design by Studiofour Graphics, Tyson's Corner, Va.

Technical Editing by Lili Bermant and Mary Daly Gorman

Printed 1977 by
AMERICAN ASSOCIATION OF COLLEGES FOR TEACHER EDUCATION
Suite 610, One Dupont Circle, Washington, D.C. 20036

Printed in the United States of America

Library of Congress Catalog Card Number: 77-78408
Standard Book Number: 0-89333-004-3

CONTENTS

Editors and Contributors   iv
Foreword   v
Preface   vi
Introduction   ix
Volume Overview   1

PART I. SCHOOLS AND TEACHING:
    A KALEIDOSCOPIC VIEW
    The Range of Schools   3
    The Variegated Nature and Status of Teaching   6
    Effect of the Larger Environment   15

PART II. SCHOOLS AS ORGANIZATIONS: THREE
    DISCUSSIONS WITH COMMENTARY
    1. Two Anomalies and Three Perspectives: Some
        Observations on Schools Organization   20
    2. Schools as Social Organizations   39
    3. Hierarchy and Egalitarianism: The Case for the
        Study of Organizations in the Education of
        Teachers—An Organizer's View   58
    4. Commentary: Some Reflections on Issues Raised in
        the Three Discussions   72

PART III. SCHOOLS AND TEACHERS IN ACTION
    Summary of Activities   81
    Draw a School   81
    Schools as Organizations   83
    John Banks: A Sequential Case Study   84
    Writing a Case Study   101
    Up the Down Staircase   105

POSTSCRIPT   108

APPENDIX: Instructional Mode, Goals, and Objectives   111

Editors and Contributors

Theodore E. Andrews, Director, Concern for Educational
   Development, Inc.
Brenda L. Bryant, Director, Concern for Educational Development, Inc.
Ronald G. Corwin, Professor of Sociology, The Ohio State University
Roy A. Edelfelt, Professional Associate, Instruction and Professional
   Development, National Education Association
Girard D. Hottleman, Assistant Executive Secretary for Programs,
   Massachusetts Teachers Association
Dan C. Lortie, Professor of Education, University of Chicago
Mark Newton, Faculty of Curriculum and Foundations, The Ohio State
   University
Melvin M. Tumin, Professor of Sociology and Anthropology, Princeton
   University

*The opinions expressed herein should not necessarily be construed as representing the
opinions of the agencies and institutions with which the editors and contributors are
affiliated.*

Foreword

The American Association of Colleges for Teacher Education and the Association of Teacher Educators are pleased to have the opportunity to publish *Perspectives on Organizations: The School as a Social Organization,* the second of three books in this series on the study of organizations. Our intent in publishing this document, in collaboration with Teacher Corps, U.S. Office of Education, is to provide ideas and information for those responsible for preparation of education personnel.

While the first volume presented a broad framework for analyzing organizations, this publication has a much narrower focus, the study of schools as organizations. Both pre- and in-service education personnel need to know more about schools as organizations. We feel that this volume addresses that need. In releasing this document, neither association necessarily endorses its content. The purpose of our serving as publishers is to stimulate study and implementation of ideas and information as appropriate for local, state, and collegiate education agencies.

Creating a publication involves many individuals. We acknowledge with gratitude the efforts of the following: Ronald G. Corwin and Roy A. Edelfelt conceptualized and wrote much of the document. Theodore E. Andrews and Brenda Bryant did much substantive editing and writing to complete the manuscript. Joel L. Burdin and Florence Jones of AACTE and Robert J. Stevenson of ATE carried out discussions which culminated in the final agreement for a cooperative publication venture. Technical editing was done by Lili Bermant and Mary Daly Gorman. None of the work could have been done without the encouragement and support of Teacher Corps Director William L. Smith, who over the years has done such an effective job in promoting American education.

Now, these efforts have reached their culmination in the publication of this volume. We believe the usefulness of this document will justify the efforts which have made it possible.

Edward C. Pomeroy, Executive Director
American Association of Colleges for
Teacher Education

Robert J. Stevenson, Executive Director
Association of Teacher Educators

June 1977

Preface

The Teacher Corps conducted its first national training institute in the summer of 1975. New project interns and team leaders, called corpsmembers, were participants in four intense weeks at the University of Richmond. In scope and content the institute was a unique response. Needs gave it birth; and evaluation studies, project directors, and research on the management of change gave it focus. The experience, known as the Corps Members Training Institute (CMTI), was repeated for other corpsmembers in 1976 at Florida State University in Tallahassee.

The major impetus for the whole idea must be credited to third-party program evaluations. More than one of these pointed up the great need for interns to understand the organizational features of schools. The Corwin Study in 1973 particularly described how crucial it was for our teaching teams, and particularly the interns, to understand the implications of organizational characteristics and realize that schools are social systems. The Marsh Study in 1974 reinforced this point.

Additionally, project directors were reporting that Teacher Corps interns needed an esprit de corps, a personal identification with the national program effort. It also seemed to directors that a common training session could be the most realistic and profound cross-cultural learning and living experience ever provided by the Teacher Corps.

Finally, the research literature on the management of change and theories on the processes of change have important implications for teacher education. The Teacher Corps program is designed to help schools and colleges effect change. In the early history of the Corps, a basic assumption existed that interns, acting as change agents, could reform the school merely with their commitment and presence. This proved to be an unrealistic and unproductive assumption. We have now been careful to insist that Teacher Corps interns are not, and should not attempt to be, change agents. Our expectation is simply that they will be the best and most highly qualified teachers available to the profession, not in the traditional sense as dispensers of knowledge, but as facilitators of the learning process. This new role requires more and different theory and training than has been the case typically in teacher education. It starts with the assumption that facilitating means managing. Teachers must manage processes, products, and young people in an organized manner if they want and expect positive growth and change to occur in the learning and behavior of their students. This seems most accomplishable when the school is viewed as a formal organization, as a social system, and the classrooms in that school as subsystems. This systemic approach treats the classroom as an organization within an organization—the school.

Previous teacher training programs, which focused on the individual teacher learner, tended to provide new knowledge or skills to that teacher learner but did not have impact for change on the school to which the teacher returned. In many cases the teacher's new knowledge became a threat to teaching peers who had not themselves benefited from such training. Administrators were often threatened when the teacher attempted to implement this new knowledge and skill. We now know how these problems can be avoided. Many of us have come to believe that for the institutionalized growth and development of educational personnel, and for impact on the school, the school as an organization is the smallest unit of change. Similarly, for the institutionalized growth and development of children, the classroom is the smallest unit of change.

Systems theory and organizational behavior theory have an important place in the conceptualization of preservice and inservice education. Many good and talented teachers feel unable to use their talents effectively because they believe the hierarchical structure of administrators, supervisors, and the environmental field force known as "the community" have placed unwarranted constraints upon them. This sense of alienation and powerlessness in the finest teachers will obviously prove contagious. Idealistic beginners will, therefore, hardly be immune. Teacher Corps is persuaded that if schools, as social systems, are to be changed for the better, everyone with a role or investment in the education and/or schooling of children must be collaboratively involved in the change process. If both new and experienced teachers were to have an opportunity to study the nature of organizations and the ways members interact, they might find that certain behavior characteristics manifested in schools are found in most organizations. Even more important, these behaviors can be understood and dealt with.

We know, of course, that most of the scientific data on organization are found in studies of economic and industrial organizations. Over the past few years, universities have conducted numerous educational organization studies in educational administration for middle managers and school superintendents, initially supported through the Kellogg Foundation Program. No one, it seemed, had begun to develop concepts, theoretical formulations, and case studies for prospective and practicing teachers to use in studying the school as a formal organization. With the exception of the initial work on organization study done by Chris Argyris for employees, little else had been developed for a role group below that of administrators and managers. Someone somewhere had to begin.

The Corps Member Training Institutes were seen as having three goals. The first was to develop an esprit de corps among our newest members. The second was to provide them with a rich multicultural experience. The third was to involve them and their experienced teacher team leader in an academic experience designed to open their eyes to theories of organization, both structure and behavior, and to the many styles of learning and teaching there are. The first Institute was organized into the two separate graduate-level strands, Organization Perspectives, and Teaching and Learning Style Analysis. This volume is the second of a series of three dealing with Perspectives on Organizations. We hope to use this series as part of the curriculum of future CMTI's.

The Teacher Corps is pleased to have the American Association of Colleges for Teacher Education and the Association of Teacher Educators serve as joint publishers of this volume. Their constituencies are important ones in any effort to implement change in the preparation of education personnel. Their effort is to provide practitioners, decision makers, and researchers with the ideas and information which can become building steps to progress.

This volume like the preceding one offers those who may share our concerns about some of the papers, other materials and procedures that were used to give corpsmembers and team leaders a new perspective on organizations particularly, as the subtitle states, on the school as a social organization.

The contents of this volume were selected from materials prepared for CMTI, 1975. Jim Steffensen and Beryl Nelson of my staff are to be commended for having worked so closely with the publication's editors on each of these volumes.

These represent beginnings, at least, of a response to a serious need. The subsequent volume of *Perspectives on Organizations* will focus on schools in their social-political contexts. Each of the three volumes reinforces the single fact that systems and organization theory are no luxury items in a realistic program of teacher training.

William L. Smith
Director
Teacher Corps

June 1977

Introduction

Consider this situation. You have recently changed residence and have applied for a telephone. The telephone company informs you by mail that a phone will be installed within the next three working days but it is not possible at this time to specify an exact time. Since you work away from home during the day, and other members of the family will not be there, you call the company to request a specific appointment so that you will be sure to be there when the installer arrives to let him/her in and to give instructions on where to locate the phone. However, the woman at the telephone company in charge of this matter informs you that she only processes the orders and has no control over the installers' schedules. You are advised not to contact the installation department directly, and in any event, you are assured, orders are filled only as they come in and are scheduled for the week.

Two weeks later you call again to report that installers have come to your home three different times but since they were not able to enter, they merely left notes indicating that fact. It is suggested that you leave a key for them somewhere, but you object: You don't know any of the neighbors, there have been burglaries in the neighborhood, you would have to take the trouble to make an extra key, and in any case, you have a fierce dog that would prohibit the installer from entering.

What might you do? How could you resolve the problem? There is no correct answer: none we can guarantee to be effective. However, we suspect that you have some ideas and that your ideas reveal a theory of organization that you hold in the back of your mind. Each of us has some such theory about how organizations function. We must have a theory in order to deal with the problems. For example, suppose that you demand to see a supervisor who is over both departments. You are thereby making an assumption about the locus of power and authority, and about the relative vulnerability of different echelons to the influence of an outsider like yourself.

Suppose instead you choose to register a personal appeal to the employee in this situation whom you originally contacted. You are then making assumptions about her autonomy—her discretion, or her ability to get around policies over which she has no official authority. We often underestimate the ingenuity of low-ranking employees. At the same time, we should allow that when an employee appears to be stubborn or indifferent, the real source is often the employer's expectations or inflexible rules that must be followed to hold one's job. Even if your estimation of the employee's discretion proves correct, you will also have to assess what leverage you have and what incentives you can offer to persuade him or her to help you. You must assess your own status; perhaps you will decide to call upon a more influential third party to intervene on your behalf. Finally, perhaps you will choose to "give up," that is, stay home for three days. Then you have acted on still other assumptions about the power of organizations in this society.

Our point is that it is imperative for each of us to formulate some tentative assumptions about organizations in order to work with them. These assumptions usually just evolve inadvertently over time, but this need not be the case. Assuming that one doesn't lose patience and will operate on reasoned thought, assumptions can be formulated, systematically tested with personal experience, and revised as seems necessary. A person who takes the trouble to do this can usually work more effectively in any organization.

Since our discussions here are directed toward school teachers, we have assumed that even those readers who are already familiar with particular schools on a day-to-day basis will wish to give further consideration to how schools are organized and how they function.

Whereas the approach taken in Volume I, *Perspectives on Organizations: Viewpoints for Teachers*, was general and intended as an introduction to gaining greater sophistication in dealing with organizations, the focus in this volume is more specifically on schools as organizations. Of course, we would not try to treat schools in isolation, even if that were possible. The school must be understood as part of the context of the community and society where it exists.

Our intent is to contribute to the thoughtfulness of teachers, not to prescribe ways of dealing with organizations. The papers chosen for this volume reflect some of the different approaches and perspectives that can be taken toward schools. The writers do not always take the same viewpoint; sometimes, they obviously disagree among themselves. In addition, we have found that readers sometimes interpret certain statements in different ways, and that any reader can misinterpret what a writer has said, because of differences in assumptions and purpose.

By dealing with controversial issues and including writers who have strong convictions, some feathers inevitably will be ruffled. Both the stark findings of research in the social sciences and the candid opinions of writers in those sciences make for lively discussion and some conflict. We consider that a positive factor necessary to stimulate thought and assertive professional action.

This second volume proceeds from the basic orientation to organizations established in Volume I. The objectives and instructional mode stated in Volume I also apply to this material and appear in the Appendix. An extensive Bibliography and Abstracts of Selected Readings included in Volume I are intended to serve all the volumes in the series.

Ronald G. Corwin, Columbus, Ohio
Roy A. Edelfelt, Washington, D.C.

June 1977

Volume Overview

This volume includes papers and other materials expressing several views on organizational problems in schools. The authors represent different persuasions about what is problematic and how to attain solutions. Of necessity, all of the authors had to focus on and thus simplify, their views somewhat; none is complete; and none is advocated as *the* view or approach to take. But taken as a set, the papers here reflect a range of thinking and perspectives on organizational problems in schools which should stretch the reader's thinking and aid him/her to arrive at an individual point of view.

In this, as in other volumes in this series, we have assumed that studying available knowledge about schools is not the sole province of administrators. Teachers also need knowledge about how schools operate, and if changes are made to improve schools they, along with parents, students, and others, must be involved. Teachers, students, and parents, are the central actors in schools, with enough power to influence and change the system in particular ways—if they recognize that fact and are equipped to act.

However, teachers often get into the profession before they realize many of the ramifications of what it means to be a professional educator. They may have been attracted to teaching by occupational aspirations, such as a personal interest in a particular subject, an interest in working with young people, or a distaste for competition in the commercial world. They probably were not fully aware of the organizational responsibilities associated with the occupation, such as living within a budget, working in an organizational hierarchy, cooperating with colleagues, working with parents and the community and initiating new programs. We hope that the materials in this book will provide another step toward helping teachers and other citizens to understand and deal more effectively with organizational problems.

This book is not designed necessarily to be read from beginning to end. Instructors and participants will, of course, read the entire book carefully. As is suggested in Part III, there are a number of strategies that might be employed to gain a full understanding of the issues raised in Parts I and II. A review of Part III will help participants and instructors decide how to approach the study of schools as organizations and how to use the materials contained in this volume.

The reader should not assume that this book or other volumes in this series will provide specific guidelines for resolving problems in schools or other organizations. We do hope, however, that the information and ideas about organizations will help substantially in the analysis and understanding of problems and conflicts, and that each reader will be more insightful in the way he or she functions in the organization— whether to influence changes or merely to cope with things as they are.

Part I
Schools and Teaching:
A Kaleidoscopic View
Ronald G. Corwin*   Roy A. Edelfelt*

In Part II of this volume there are papers in which authors concentrate on particular aspects of schools. It is convenient, and often necessary, to aim discussion to the average school and the typical features of teaching. A reader could become hopelessly confused, and this book would be voluminous, if every author tried to take into account every contingency that could arise, given the wide spectrum of schools and occupational characteristics. Having said that about the discussions to come, it is helpful initially to address the big picture, to consider the diverse and variegated nature of our subject. We shall proceed then, to address (a) the range of schools, (b) the multifaceted nature of teaching, and (c) the complications that arise because schools are part of a larger sociohistorical environment.

THE RANGE OF SCHOOLS

Schools are rudimentary bureaucracies. They have many of the features that make up bureaucratic organizations: hierarchies, rules, close supervision, specialization, et cetera. However, simply labeling them as "bureaucracies" obscures the wide differences among them. In practice, there is not just one form of "bureaucracy"; it can take many forms for different purposes. Some forms prove better than others. In Volume I, a distinction was made between a "bureaucracy," which refers to a very specific structural pattern, and a "complex" organization, which can assume a variety of patterns. For example, even very large school districts can differ in the degree to which decisions are decentralized, curricula are standardized, teachers are professionalized, and the like. We suggest that schools should be regarded as complex organizations which, in some instances, assume bureaucratic proportions.

Our first point, then, is that most schools are not uniform. Think of a large city ghetto school, patrolled by police, poorly maintained, with peeling paint, concrete playground, high rates of truancy and delinquency, and a big bureaucracy, staffed by callous teachers. Contrast such a school with a new, modern campus school, set in a

*We thank each of the authors who have contributed papers to this volume for reading and making helpful comments on "Schools and Teaching: A Kaleidoscopic View."

wooded area, carpeted and painted in bright colors, servicing largely middle class, well-dressed students, with a faculty of enthusiastic, responsive people. These are obviously exaggerated and stereotyped portrayals, but they help remind us of the differences that can be found among schools.

Still other differences can be observed between public and private schools, and between elementary, junior high and high schools. The objectives of vocational schools seem clearer than those of comprehensive schools; compulsory attendance is a serious constraint in some schools and almost irrelevant in others; students are regimented in some schools and given a great deal of autonomy in others. The list could go on almost indefinitely.

This range of differences is compounded by the complexity of the educative system itself. Consider for example, the matter of local control. Although local school boards do have authority over some important matters, state departments of education retain final authority over basic curricula, athletic programs, certification of teachers, school construction, bonding programs, and a host of other key decisions. Also, although the federal government provides a relatively small proportion of the total costs of education, it has influenced several major curricular changes and altered social policies, including racial integration and busing. Teacher organizations also influence policy and practice through their many activities at local, state and national levels. Then, too, in a mobile society even decisions made by local school boards will be strongly influenced by developments in the major industrial centers where students find jobs. Is education more, or less, locally controlled than community hospitals, police departments, or libraries?

Given the existing diversity among schools, it is necessary to stress a second point. One should be very cautious in comparing schools with other organizations such as hospitals, churches or factories. If there are more differences than similarities between a one-room school house and a high school in a large city, for example, then it may be more appropriate to compare the big-city schools to big-city hospitals, churches or factories than to rural schools. In any case, it is not clear that there are major differences between schools and other organizations, or that schools are so unique they must be studied in isolation from other kinds of organizations.

What does it mean to say that schools are unique anyway? Too often it depends upon what is being compared. For example, some schools permit employees more autonomy than some hospitals, but probably less than many universities. The cellular classroom structure of schools notwithstanding, some teachers, in some places are closely supervised. A good rule of thumb is to recognize that schools consist of the same set of variables as any other organization. What varies is the profile of variables, i.e., the degree of emphasis, or ranking, of particular variables. It is important to look at it in this way, because one then continues to examine the same variables for schools as for other organizations, and research on other organizations continues to be relevant for understanding schools. Such an approach precludes the conclusion that schools are so different from other organizations that general knowledge about organizations has no relevance for understanding schools. That premise will only reinforce an already parochial conventional wisdom about schools.

A good example of what can happen when schools are treated as uniform among themselves and uniquely different from other institutions is illustrated in the accountability movement. In recent years some critics have pressed their demands that schools, and teachers in particular, should be more accountable to the public. In practice, "accountability" has usually been equated with achieving uniform outcomes that are unique to schools, as measured by standardized test scores. In this preoccupation with test scores, the nature of schools as variable and complex social systems, sharing certain features with other organizations, has been grossly oversimplified and distorted. Because they are limited to results, tests scores obscure universal organizational factors that underlie the recruitment of students and the process of schooling.

A potentially promising alternative is to measure school climates, the customs, values, norms, and organizational roles and procedures that underlie any social system. Take the following for example:

Scope of the Norms and Values

As in any social system, in a school there is room for individuals to use their own discretion in some matters (alternative norms), but they are also expected to conform to general expectations which apply either to all members of the organization (universals), or to specific positions and responsibilities (specific norms). The amount of consensus on each type of norm also can vary. These norms and values pertain to the objectives of the school, the acceptability of and priority given to various courses of study (citizenship and political awareness), the emphasis placed on student conduct (discipline), creativity, extracurricular activities, scholarship in the fundamentals, test performance and the like. These norms and values are also reflected in the actual criteria and sanctions used to evaluate and reward members of the organization. The norms might be grouped into several broad categories, i.e., organizational, political, social psychological, intellectual, etc.

Participants

Viewed as a social system, a school includes several different groups, all of which share responsibility for it: teachers, students, administrators, and community members (school board members, informal leaders, and organized groups concerned with schools).

System Components

Finally, the outcomes of any social system can be understood as products of a complex chain of factors, including:

- "Inputs," or the ability or motivation of students admitted to the school, available resources, and training of personnel. This includes the tax base, type of students, use of specialists and administrators, and the number, experience, and training of teachers.
- "Throughput," or the availability of specialized programs, types of materials, and sophistication of technology and teaching procedures used.
- "Structure," or the coordination procedures used to integrate the system, including type of supervision, numbers of rules and procedures for enforcing rules, use of standardized procedures, locus of decision-making, and mechanisms for appealing decisions.

Teaching and learning, in other words, are shaped by these and other related characteristics of the school's organization. It is unrealistic to consider the outcome without also taking into account the school's ability to select its students and teachers, and the programs and resources available. Any analysis that concentrates on only a few of the many factors involved can be completely misleading. Focusing on the total system (instead of test scores) will deepen understanding of the schooling process. The possibility of scapegoating, i.e., blaming teachers, or students, or parents for organizational inadequacies will be minimized. Problems (or lack of them) will be correctly seen as functions of the organization. Parents, students, teachers, and administrators will better understand why their school is what it is and perhaps will see how they can contribute to its improvement.

Therefore, while it may often be necessary to gloss over the enormous variability in the characteristics of schools, we should remain cognizant of them. They are bound to modify any general conclusions we may reach.

THE VARIEGATED NATURE AND STATUS OF TEACHING

The multidimensional status system that underlies teaching as an occupation also complicates the analysis of schools. The term, status, refers to the ways in which individuals and groups are ranked within a society, occupation, or organization. Three features of status systems are important for this discussion.

First, status can be assigned (and perceived) by either the general society or a subgroup within the society. Teachers, or some other group, might rank teaching differently than is reflected in general public opinion.

Second, the status of an occupation can differ from the status of

6

individuals in it. One can make an important distinction between the status attributes of individual teachers—their education and the like—and the importance of their role in society.

Third, status is determined by a number of factors, including its importance to the society, power, autonomy, income, prestige, sophistication of specialized knowledge, and technology. We will give further consideration to some of these dimensions.

Power and Authority

The authority of teachers, that is their right to prevail by virtue of their formal rank, is defined by their position in the school district hierarchy. On this dimension, teachers rank relatively low in comparison to school administrators. However this authority rank is only one form of power, and they do have other sources of power. For example, they can claim the right to prevail on the basis of their expertise, i.e., their demonstrated excellence in a particular field, expertise in pedagogy, and their detailed information about particular students or about children of a given age. Discrepancies between authority from rank and authority from expertise often produce conflict in schools. For example, suppose that most of the science teachers in a school system object to a textbook that has been required for all students by the superintendent's office, or by the state board of education. These teachers will presume that they have something to contribute to decisions about teaching materials, and chances are, if they are insistent enough and if they flex their collective muscle, they will at least be given a hearing.

Many readers will probably question the reasonableness of entrusting decisions about classroom materials to administrative nonspecialists who will never use them. Others might feel that it is equally inappropriate to leave such decisions entirely to specialists who are not directly accountable to the parents. These are the very questions that underlie controversies about the propriety of sex education, for example. The reader might wish to ponder how teachers can be protected from the poor judgments of administrators in such matters, and how a reasonable mix can be reached between command, authority and expertise.

Such conflicts are often resolved through power struggles, i.e., one group imposing its will on another. It is possible for an individual or group to seize unauthorized power, and so, we can say that there is a hierarchy of power distinct from the authority hierarchies just referred to. Although teachers rank low in the hierarchical authority system, they can nevertheless gain power through collective action. But, the unresolved question is whether that power can be transformed into authority, and justified by expertise. Might does not always make right. And expertise does not always prevail.

Teacher organizations provide a power base for teachers. Collective action can help offset the relatively low authority accorded to each individual teacher within the school hierarchy. However, there is a catch.

Labor unions and professional associations are themselves organized as hierarchies. Therefore, teacher organizations do not necessarily minimize hierarchy or improve the position of most teachers within it. Most members will simply find themselves at the bottom of another hierarchy, where they have little more power as individuals than they do in the school district as a whole.

In addition to the fact that the teachers' unfavorable position in the hierarchy can be compensated for in other ways, the inevitability of hierarchy itself can be questioned. A hierarchy is a way of organizing. It is a means to an end. A hierarchical decision-making structure can be very efficient when the organization is operated on a rational model with clear goals. Theoretically the person at the top is held responsible and makes quick, informed decisions that are passed along to specialists to implement. However, this assumes that the goals are known and shared. But, suppose the organization is an organic type in which there is disagreement about which goals to pursue, i.e., the goals advocated by the administration are questioned by subordinates. In such a case, efficiency must be subordinated to the prior task of setting the goals. Hierarchy is not necessarily effective for this purpose. What is needed for such situations is a form of organization that maximizes participation and negotiation; one that permits conflict within bounds; one that provides a way of regulating conflict and reaching compromise.

There are several alternatives to hierarchy. Decentralization is one alternative that is often recommended. Of course, even in a decentralized organization, some decisions remain centralized while others are delegated; e.g., equipment purchases often are made at the central office while decisions about which textbooks to purchase are made at the building level. Nevertheless, coupled with neighborhood citizens' advisors, this type of flat hierarchy could increase the responsiveness of a school district to the conditions of different types of neighborhoods.

There are also other alternatives. For example, decisions could be made at the top by committees consisting of representatives of a wide range of groups; individuals could rotate into and out of the top position; or procedures could be developed by which subordinates could appeal the decisions with which they disagree. Perhaps the reader can think of still other alternatives.

However, it is not clear that organizations would become radically different even if alternatives to the hierarchy were found. Does it necessarily follow that schools would become more flexible if teachers got more power? Such an assumption fails to take into consideration the fundamental reasons why conservatism arises in organizations. It is not just a question of personality, and conservatism is not confined to administrators. While the top officials may be preoccupied with stability, it is also evident that teachers at subordinate levels often resist changes that are introduced from the top. Perhaps the underlying consideration is that conservatism is a way of adapting to the job insecurities felt by individuals who are committed to their jobs when they are left with few employment options and find themselves faced with uncertainties and little incentive to take risks. Unless these conditions are changed, it is entirely likely that conservatism will simply follow power, and that if power is decentralized, subordinates might become as conservative as administrators are often said to be. The implication is clear. If teacher organizers want change, they will first have to negotiate for alterations in these conditions. Getting more power for teachers is not sufficient.

Power, then, is an important dimension of status. Indeed, increasingly, the equation that spells status includes both money and power. Teachers have been successful in getting both through collective action. However, they may miss the full equation of status if these are the only two purposes of collective action. They may also destroy their image with the public and become regarded as self-serving and unconcerned with the welfare of students. Teacher groups in the most advanced stages of collective bargaining (e.g., Massachusetts, New Jersey, Michigan) recognize this problem and are trying to deal with it in their collective bargaining practices.

Autonomy

Teachers also have a great deal of autonomy, i.e., discretion, because they typically work in self-contained classrooms behind closed doors and are seldom formally observed or evaluated by their superiors. They can select materials, develop their own teaching methods, choose which content to stress or to slight, schedule classroom activities, and enforce discipline policies rigidly or loosely.

However, it is easy to overestimate the importance of teacher autonomy. For, no matter how much autonomy teachers may appear to have, particularly over classroom matters, their options are still limited by their college training, tradition, rules, standardized procedures, public opinion, laws, accrediting agencies, their own peers and professional associations, and their own lack of initiative. For example, often teachers must keep in mind that their students will be evaluated against standardized tests, and they usually are not permitted to omit material that is supposed to be covered at a particular grade level. Classroom methods that upset some parents, or that subject the school to public criticism, are likely to bring reprisals from school administrators. Indeed, classrooms can provide a false sense of security. They can isolate teachers from the larger context, shield them from understanding the system-wide problems, and discourage them from becoming involved even in decisions that ultimately affect their own classrooms.

We also should be careful not to stereotype schools in this, as in other respects. If the teacher's autonomy stems from the self-contained classroom, it is instructive that in a recent study of 28 schools, W. W.

Charters and his colleagues at the University of Oregon found that less than one half of the teachers in these schools taught in self-contained classrooms. In fact, there were only a few schools where all teachers taught in self-contained classrooms. Equally striking variations were found in other characteristics that were compared. It should be recognized that the sample for the Charters study was not selected randomly and that cooperation (teaming) among teachers reported in that study was largely informal. In any event cooperation could be disrupted by administrative decisions, transfers or changes in grade-level assignments.

The extent to which structural looseness, and thus the autonomy of teachers varies from school to school depends upon the kind of coordinating mechanisms used and whether there are procedures that permit joint decision making and collective action. Also, areas in which discretion is permitted change over time. For example, although theoretically the curriculum probably has been relatively free from rules, in recent years it has come under tighter control with the development of "competency based education" and "management by objectives." Indeed, schools are probably much more tightly coordinated than universities. The looseness or tightness of control is one element of variation that is seldom emphasized by organizational theorists, but it is of obvious importance for understanding schools as organizations.

Social Importance

Some sociologists maintain that an occupation's status rewards can be explained by the occupation's importance, in other words, its contribution to the society. One sometimes detects this assumption on the part of individuals or groups seeking to justify the demands of doctors, lawyers or teachers for higher income, prestige or other rewards. Perhaps the function performed by members of an occupation does have something to do with their status, but we are skeptical about such arguments. In the first place, we doubt that status rewards are distributed as logically or equitably as this line of reasoning implies. Even if it were agreed, for example, that teachers deserve more recognition, merit is only one factor in their actual ability to command status rewards.

In the second place, even if it were agreed that some functions like protecting health or civil rights or overseeing socialization of the young were more important than others (e.g., flying commercial airliners), the fact is that no one occupation can claim major responsibility for such functions. For example, teaching cannot be equated with "education" nor can education be equated with "socialization." True, the way people are socialized shapes society, and formal education (along with family and peer group, and mass media) is partly responsible for socialization, but teachers are only a small part of the larger culture, the school system, and the school district, all of which set expectations (and limits) for the teacher role. It is an exaggeration, an overextension, therefore, to say that the formal teaching role, as it is institutionalized in school systems, is primarily responsible for the shape of society.

Income

In the U.S. (and other Western nations) income is an important consideration. If the average medical doctor earns about $200 a day, compared to about $60 for a teacher (based on a ten-month year), the teacher obviously has lower status according to this criterion. Although teachers' salaries are favored over the average of all wage and salary workers, and their earnings now compare favorably with those of nurses, civil servants of the federal government still out-earn teachers; and the starting salaries for engineers exceed those of teachers by nearly twenty-five percent (based on a ten-month year for teachers).

Prestige

The prestige of teaching as an occupation has fluctuated only slightly in years, and it is still a highly regarded occupation. A more than three-fold increase in the numbers of teachers since 1940 has perhaps blurred the distinctiveness of being a teacher. Also, occupations in research, technology, communications and other services previously not available to the workforce now compete with teaching. Moreover, the education differential between teachers and the general population, while still favorable to teachers, has declined slightly as more high school graduates enter institutions of higher education. Nevertheless, it is telling that the prestige of teaching, as reflected in public opinion surveys, appears to have increased since World War II.

Specialized Knowledge

Questions also can be raised about whether the knowledge base of teaching has improved. Some sociologists think of teachers as generalists, and perhaps they are, especially at the elementary school level. However, teachers are becoming more specialized than many people have recognized.

The prevalence of specialized roles within teaching is reflected in the nearly 100,000 employed librarians, guidance personnel, psychological personnel, and other nonsupervisory instructional personnel who are neither employed in classroom nor in supervisory-administrative positions. Moreover, since the teacher shortage has abated, the practice of assigning teachers to teach in areas outside of their major has become less prevalent, and the practice of hiring teachers with provisional certificates has almost disappeared. At the same time, team teaching and differentiated staffing could force school systems to use teachers in more specialized ways, and perhaps multi-unit, ungraded schools and open-concept schools will permit more individualized programs consonant with the application of specialized technologies for different types of clientele. Also, it might be noted that the proportion of elementary schools that are departmentalized has increased four-fold in the past decade (from five percent in 1961 to 21 percent in 1971).

As a result of these various forms of specialization, the traditional role the line administrator has played as "curriculum leader" probably became unfeasible in many instances years ago. Although administrators are still responsible for evaluating the competence of teachers in different pedagogical techniques and subject matter areas, the time may be rapidly approaching when it will not be possible for administrators to assume the exclusive responsibility for evaluating teachers.

The growth of specialized interests within teaching (which might reflect some increase in specialized knowledge as well) is indicated in the number of journals that deal with special aspects of teaching. (See the *International Periodicals Dictionary*.) Since 1961, 73 new journals have been added, 31 of them since 1966. There are now nearly 150 publications dealing with varied aspects of teaching. Of those added during the past decade, at least 37 appear to deal with specialized subject matter; only seven have general titles, ten are regional, and six are both specialized and regional.

Special interests are also reflected in the innumerable teacher organizations that exist in the country. There are more than three dozen organizations for teachers and numerous organizations for school administrators, many at one time affiliated with the National Education Association (NEA). The *Education Directory* lists approximately two dozen independent associations and councils that explicitly deal with specialized problems in teaching. These organizations range from the National Council of Teachers of English and an association for kindergarten teachers, to the American Association of School Librarians and the American Montessori Society. There are several associations concerned with the education of various kinds of handicapped or gifted children, with guidance and counseling, and with vocational, technical, and adult education. There are also numerous national and regional organizations for teachers in specialized subject matter areas, including math and science, English, business, vocal and instrumental music, chemistry and languages. A National League of Teachers' Associations is also listed.

Technology

By comparison to medicine, perhaps teaching does not seem to have highly developed, sophisticated technology, if one defines technology as the means of getting a job done. Technological competence usually rests on the extent to which the theoretical bases of technology have been codified, and teaching is still carried on primarily according to uncodified rules, accumulative experience, and lore. Effective techniques for maintaining classroom control, motivating children, and conveying information are not well developed or standardized. Flaws and considerable variation can be cited in micro-teaching, team teaching, nongraded schooling, new math, the initial teaching alphabet, and other technological innovations. There is no evidence that any of these innovations are more effective than traditional technologies.

Perhaps such criteria are too stringent. A few specialized techniques and tools are now available for teaching subjects like math, spelling and reading, for working with handicapped and academically advanced children, and for coping with problems of low-income schools. Performance-based teacher education is a comparatively unproven and controversial attempt to identify competencies and skills needed by teachers and to require that prospective teachers demonstrate that these skills have been acquired as a condition for certification.

The fact that various new technologies are available probably has an important bearing on the progress of the occupation as a whole, irrespective of their often indeterminate effectiveness and lack of widespread use. Moreover, the standard of reference used in discussions preoccupied with the question of whether or not teaching is "really a profession" in some absolute sense should be the amount and direction of change that has occurred within teaching in recent decades, not the comparison between teaching and other occupations so often implicit in these discussions.

Finally, we should note that some teachers dispute, or at least equivocate about, the importance of technology for teaching, arguing that teaching is an art which should be judged on the basis of the intuitive abilities and creativity of teachers in the profession, not on scientific criteria. There are problems with this argument, too. One is that parents usually look for "results" (i.e., observable learning outcomes). Unless the artful teacher can out-perform others on this measure, he or she will be downgraded. Also, it seems more difficult to socialize the thousands of new teachers who enter teaching each year to practice the relative mysterious art of teaching than it is to train them to use its more straightforward (if sometimes complex) technologies. Technology provides an element of standardization, and hence assurance, that many school boards demand. Ideally, it would be preferable to recognize that teaching is both a science and an art. However, it is no simple task to strike an appropriate balance, to employ modern technology without discouraging the intuitive and creative approaches.

The Quality of Professional Life

For at least some teachers, undoubtedly the main consideration is the degree to which their work is intellectually stimulating and emotionally rewarding. Some of these individuals seem willing to accept relatively low pay or prestige if they can maintain satisfying work relationships with colleagues, parents and students.

An intellectually stimulating and emotionally rewarding teaching assignment is often difficult to achieve, however. For, as an occupation gains autonomy, and because of the very nature of autonomy, the practitioners tend to become isolated from the clientele and other outside groups. Teacher organizations try to protect teachers from parents and their students in addition to defending their interests with administrators and school boards, and in the process they isolate the teachers from these outside clients. Since the clients of a profession do not have enough training and experience to assess professional performance accurately, their opinions can be discounted or ignored by the professionals. Often, achievement standards applicable to all students are set regardless of individual circumstances. This can seem like indifference, which can create especially severe problems in public organizations like schools where neither the professional teacher nor the student client has much choice in entering the relationship (a condition which probably should be reexamined by teachers.

Some critics have asked whether teachers are personally interested in their students, but in the final analysis this is not the only important question. A more basic consideration is whether teachers are professionally motivated to protect students from the worst features of educational bureaucracies. For example, they must protect students from pressures in the community that threaten professional norms, that favor an outmoded curriculum, or that jeopardize the students' civil rights. To the extent that professionalism provides an alternative to the local system of administration, at least there is a possibility that teachers will act as a positive force, on behalf of all students, irrespective of whether they develop personal relationships with individual students.

Bureaucratization

It has not been easy for teachers to attain professional status within large scale, bureaucratic organizations, where they are not treated solely as "professionals," since they are employees. As subordinate employees, they must learn to cope with complex and often inconsistent expectations associated with being *both* a professional and an employee. To appreciate the dilemmas this can pose, consider how some of the main features of a bureaucratic organization can affect professionalism.

As bureaucratic employees, teachers are expected to subscribe or conform to the expectations of the administration and the community. But, as professionals, teachers are expected to defend the welfare of students against organizational practices that, in their professional judgment, are likely to be detrimental. To illustrate, professional teachers will be disposed toward supporting school consolidation while opposing citizens who argue for local control. Also, while some parents attempt to protect their children from the raw realities depicted by American authors such as Steinbeck or Faulkner, professional teachers will defend the rights of students to read such authors and will adjust their teaching to the unique capabilities of their students rather than succumb to the premise that all students must cover the same textbook and be up to grade level in achievement. Depending on how their choices are made, it is possible for teachers to be successful as employees while failing to fulfill professional obligations, or vice versa. In addition consider the situation in which administrators supervise and evaluate professional subordinates who are more competent in their work than they. This situation, in turn, raises such questions as whether the criteria for reward should be loyalty to the organization, or professional skill and competence; the latter is difficult for nonspecialized administrators to evaluate. Still another problem is deciding how to deal with loyalty and competence when the typical criteria for salary are experience and formal education. The problem of evaluation is complicated and probably demands some standardization because, with teachers' reputations at stake, the opinions of colleagues outside the organization must be taken into account.

Then, too, standardization poses problems. While it is not necessarily incompatible with individualism, it can discourage creative and original thought, which is so necessary if organizations are to adapt to changing environments. But from the short-run perspective in which administrators and workers see their daily problems, predictability and consistency often appear safer and more prudent than change and the risk of applying new ideas.

EFFECT OF THE LARGER ENVIRONMENT

The fact that each school system has a unique history and social environment adds still other complications that should be kept in mind when considering organizational characteristics.

The Historical Environment

The structure of schools evolved during an era when relatively simple, hierarchical military and industrial organizations served as the model for most organizations. This pattern, deeply embedded in tradition, has been slow to change. The tendency has been to add new responsibilities to the traditional duties of teachers without the support of new staffing patterns, special training and other structural reforms. Consequently, school administrators and teachers are burdened with responsibilities they are not prepared to handle. Teachers are supposed to be prepared in a variety of specialized subjects, as well as: provide more personal guidance to students in a society that does not agree on basic values; supervise an expanding number of extracurricular activities; counsel children and parents on diverse problems (ranging from child abuse and drugs, to pregnancy and career education); and assume administrative chores connected with meal service, emergency preparedness, and the like.

The rise of organized teacher militancy makes sense against this backdrop. It is evident teachers are feeling the pinch not only because of the low pay, added work, and the routine of their jobs, but also because their authority has not kept pace with the responsibilities that have been thrust upon them. They have been omitted from the decision-making.

While history is an invaluable tool, social scientists are sometimes so awed by the power of history that they develop a fatalistic attitude toward what they see as the inevitability and immutability of historical events. This "historical imperative" often leads to pessimistic conclusions about schools and the possibility of changing their worst features. However, historical forces seem less awesome if one looks at units smaller than school districts or society as a whole. It seems more feasible to improve a particular school or school district than to try to deal with all school districts or "society" at large, and it can be hoped that attention to particular organizations can act as levers for larger changes. Moreover, change does not necessarily take place in a linear way. That is, the trend toward large scale, centralized school systems could level off or even reverse itself under several conditions: if technology is developed to permit more efficient operation of small units; if management procedures call for more participation in decision making; or if professionalization reaches the point where there is greater trust and greater assurance that responsibilities can be delegated.

We should remember how rapidly the school systems of America have developed in the last 75 years, how rapidly the population has grown, how many more students there are in schools, how many teachers have been prepared, how the percentage of adolescents attending high school has increased. Given the dynamic, restless, and cosmopolitan character this country has assumed in recent decades, the historical past is probably less important as a force on education. In any event, it is difficult to be pessimistic when one looks at that fantastic growth and still recognizes that schools are better, teachers are better educated, materials have improved.

The Larger Society

To the extent that schools are resistant to change in response to new conditions, the fast pace of change and the heterogeneity of the society creates problems. Although it should not be assumed that students are homogeneous enough to be treated uniformly, that is precisely the assumption underlying standardized textbooks and curriculum guides, the proscribed length of the school year, basic minimum requirements, uniform certification requirements for teachers, and other elements of standardization in American education.

The complicating factor, it is argued, is that in a mobile nation, all students in all parts of the country might need similar skills to compete successfully and to permit transfer from one school district to another. Thus, the argument goes, schools must be standardized to some degree, even though at the same time, they must remain responsive to cultural diversity. In practice, however, schools have not been particularly successful in their attempts to force people to fit the same mold or to progress at the same pace. Standardized tests demonstrate great variance in students within grades in the same school. In schools where students represent a normal distribution of the population, the range of achievement is about equal to the number of the grade in which the student is enrolled, i.e., a five year difference in the fifth grade, a nine year difference in the ninth grade.

Thus, the compelling pressure to standardize notwithstanding, schools have found it necessary to adjust to individual differences and to remain sensitive to unique local circumstances. Where they have not done so, outside groups often called it to the attention of school authorities, and if necessary, exerted pressure to bring about the desired changes. Thus, there will inevitably be some tension between schools, which are charged with protecting standards, and groups of citizens who require special attention.

Many observers have called attention to the fact that parents and children do not often see eye to eye. What is probably more important is the fact that teachers and parents often do not see eye to eye. Parents exercise a critical surveillance role on behalf of their children. The democratic issue is how to strengthen participation and improve the responsibility of citizens to monitor schools. This in turn requires finding a better balanced integration between schools and families that can offset some of the bureaucratic impersonality, size and inflexibility of schools.

Many of the same organizational characteristics we have been considering can isolate schools from the wishes of their clientele. For example, *bureaucratization* could tend to circumscribe interaction between teachers and parents, and establish highly impersonal and routine types of relationships. The more rigid the organizational controls, the more likely that teachers will conform to the organizational rules and authority system, which will reduce their ability to respond to the demands of parents that run counter to those rules. *Centralization* can also isolate teachers from outside contact, for if there is a problem, parents will go to the administrator who has the authority. Conversely, decentralization produces more points of contact and possibly more latitude to respond to requests on an individual basis. Teaching experience can have the same effect. The longer teachers live in a particular community, the more social contact they are likely to have with parents.

Professional training can also have isolating effects. Professionalization has often been criticized for this very reason. Socialization into an occupation which has a distinct culture often promotes "a culture gap" between the professionals and their publics. Also, training can have a cosmopolitanizing influence, which turns the professional's loyalties away from the local community. The better trained professionals have more opportunities to escape physically from problem-ridden communities and gravitate to organizations where there is less need to interact with the community. Even teacher organizations can be a factor. With strong organizations to back them up, teachers might be more inclined to work with powerful community groups, and as a result become less vulnerable to parents demanding special favors or quick solutions to problems for which there are no routine solutions.

We obviously have not considered all of the social, occupational and organizational factors that create variety in the schools of this country, but, perhaps enough has been said to illustrate some ways in which schools differ in their sensitivity and receptivity to outside influences. Each of us should be on guard against stereotyping and overgeneralizing about them as we attempt to analyze them, cope with them, and improve them.

Part II
Schools As Organizations:
Three Discussions with Commentary

In "Schools as Organizations: Three Discussions with Commentary" Dan C. Lortie, Melvin Tumin, and Girard Hottleman provide the reader with various perspectives on schools. In approach, attitude, and substance, the authors challenge teachers to consider and reassess their individual and collective roles and behaviors.

In the first discussion, "Two Anomalies and Three Perspectives," Dan Lortie introduces Part II with a lucid and balanced analysis of some fundamentals of school organization. He describes similarities and differences between schools and other organizations. The author conveys a good feel for the complexities, and some of the issues, underlying organizations that make this field challenging and often controversial.

Lortie displays a degree of working familiarity with school teaching that is rare among social scientists. He is no apologist nor is he an advocate or a reformer. The reader will find an outstanding scholar taking a dispassionate look at schools. The reader will also find a person who is empathic with teachers and appreciative of their problems.

Whereas Lortie focuses largely on the internal features of school organization, Melvin Tumin in "Schools as Social Organizations," steps back to place schools in a broader perspective. After identifying some of the problems inherent to an organizational society, he stresses the many positive contributions that large-scale organizations have made to modern societies, concluding that they are an integral feature of such societies. He also helps to illuminate the critical role that social conflict is likely to play if bureaucracies are to be made responsive to the democratic political process.

A highly respected sociologist and educator, Tumin is also a humanist. His warm compassion for the underdog—minorities, down-and-outers, youth, and neophytes—is expressed in friendly advice to new teachers. The wisdom which he shares on how to survive the first years in the profession may provide a sobering, practical antidote for a few eager, youthful teachers who might be impatient for immediate educational reform.

Girard Hottleman's remarks in "Hierarchy and Egalitarianism," stand in stark contrast with the other two discussions. He is neither dispassionate scholar nor disinterested observer. He is an intensely concerned practitioner, a spokesman for many teachers, and an advocate of change. He not only offers a theory of change, but he also is prepared to deal with the mechanics of implementing it. He attempts to cut through the complexities, to expose the simple reality, which he believes to be the fundamental conflict between teachers and their superiors in the hierarchy. His approach is provocative.

In Part III, Activity 2, the instructor is provided with some suggested exercises for introducing the three papers to and discussing them with participants. It is suggested that the reader review the exercises prior to reading Part II.

Section 1: Two Anomalies and Three Perspectives: Some Observations on School Organization

Dan C. Lortie

We probably should not be surprised when teachers show little interest in the organizational aspects of teaching. The psychological center of teaching, after all, lies in the classroom where teachers encounter their major challenges and reap their most valued rewards (Lortie, 1975). Taken seriously, teaching does not leave much extra energy for what seem to be remote questions of school operation. Forays into organizational affairs (for example, committee service) often reinforce teacher doubts about such efforts; it is not uncommon for veterans to tell how protracted work, assiduously performed, produced no discernible effect. The inclination of most teachers is to "delegate" organizational matters to administrators or to those few colleagues who obviously enjoy them.

However such indifference may have affected teaching in the past, it may be that avoidance of such engagements will prove costly in the future. That possibility rests on two current trends—the initiation and expansion of collective bargaining and the emerging research-and-development frame of mind. Because teachers have been somewhat insulated from their settings in the past, they have been able to afford their detachment. Both of the trends mentioned, however, are likely to reduce the insulation.

Collective bargaining is, of course, an important change in teaching work. Like other important changes, it brings consequences that few people expected. Its success has reduced the publicly perceived innocence of teachers and increased public readiness to impose sharper and higher standards of performance. For to the degree that teachers collectively participate in the centers of power and decision making, they share blame as well as credit for the state of education. Furthermore, collective action produces collective counter-assertions, as we see in widespread demands for teacher accountability. American society seems to be saying, "Now that we pay you more, we expect more." None of this is to gainsay the benefits that teachers have obtained through joint assertiveness. However, this very success, as early proponents predicted, has changed the status of teachers; the ritual pity of the past, lamentations for "our underpaid teachers," has yielded to a more vigorous image of teachers as active in the world of political action and tough bargaining. This image, in assuming that teachers are looking after their own interests, reduces the obligation felt by others to do it for them.

The "research-and-development frame of mind" is part of a broader shift taking place in American education. To quote Bagehot (1948), we are witnessing cracks in the "cake of custom." Fewer people today believe that there is a single best way to design a school building, construct a curriculum, define teachers' tasks, etc.; there are more and more options available for many facets of school life. Nor are these alternative ways of doing things purely Utopian, for many have powerful backing by influential groups such as business corporations, state departments of education, federal agencies, and large universities. Although it is new on the educational scene, instructional research and development is already producing new practices that confront school people with the necessity for choice. Plans have moved into realization as some school districts offer alternative programs, install computer-assisted instruction, use program budgets, create new arrangements for community participation, and team and differentiate teachers. It is important to note that these are not cosmetic alterations—they reach into the conduct of instruction (for example, see the May 1975 issue of *Phi Delta Kappan*). They not only challenge conventional ways of thinking about classroom affairs; they question the historic definition of the teacher's role. Members of the teaching profession may see their core activities reshaped by others. To ignore that possibility is to increase the risk that the reshaping will not be to their liking.

It is for reasons such as these, that the writer believes teachers should become more involved in studying, and influencing, the organization of school work. More than enlightened self-interest is at stake; educational values are also involved. To the extent that teachers see themselves as particularly concerned with instructional values, to that extent ought they to contribute to what is happening in the schools.

Effective action will require sophistication about how schools work. I hope that this paper helps in that respect and that it will stimulate at least some readers to further study and analysis. The organization of the paper is really self-evident: It is divided into two major sections, the first on anomalies and the second on specific comparisons of schools with other kinds of organizations. It focuses primarily on the position of teachers in schools.

TWO ANOMALIES

As formal organizations, schools and school systems share some characteristics with hospitals, factories, savings and loan associations, hotels, armies, churches, and other institutions. But schools are also special, displaying a combination of qualities found nowhere else.

Schools and school systems fit into an intricate network of educational activities in local, state, and federal governments, institutions of higher education, testing organizations, accreditation groups, the court system, taxpayers' associations, international unions, and chambers of commerce, to list only some. This network is sufficiently complex that we find special fields of study devoted to it; it is examined by educational economists, historians, sociologists, political scientists, and anthropologists. Yet schools, from another vantage point, are "simple" organizations, being essentially a collection of classrooms where individual teachers work, largely alone and for long stretches of time, with groups of students. All else seems superfluous when compared with the basic activities of learning and teaching.

Similar but unique; complex but simple. We turn now to these two anomalies in the organizational reality of public education.

Anomaly Number 1: The Shared and the Unique

Formal organizations are repetitive engagements of persons who are organized to attain specified purposes and who act in formal roles to do so. Organizational work is divided—and then coordinated—in the hope that tasks will be done in regular, predictable, and integrated ways. In schools, for example, different parties make general policy, write curriculum outlines, teach mathematics, and sit for examination. The basis for participation can include voluntary effort (board members), payment (administrators, teachers, custodians), and legal requirement and general social expectations for persons of a certain age (students).

Achieving the coordination of people assigned to different roles (particularly when they identify themselves with different occupations) is not automatic; it requires mechanisms to bring it about. One of the major means used to attain functional unity is a system of authority that formalizes decision-making and distributes the right to command and the duty to obey. In school districts, the pattern is a familiar one: A board has overall jurisdiction, administrators have managerial powers, and teachers are in charge of students. Authority follows vertical lines, and the distribution of roles takes the form of a pyramid.

Although this is not the place for a detailed discussion of the nature of formal authority systems, we should note that general statements can be made about such systems and that such knowledge is useful to persons trying to understand any particular formal organization. The exercise of authority, for example, is normally problematic both for those who exercise it and for those on the receiving end. Getting compliances with an order is not a surefire thing, for there are important conditions to be met before even the most official, authoritative order can or will be obeyed (Barnard, 1938). The reception of authority has its own complications. For example, subordinates in a wide variety of settings are usually very sensitive to issues of equity and questions of distributive justice. It matters little, in this regard, whether they are a group of vice presidents in a corporation, engineers building a system for space exploration, or sixth graders reacting to their teacher's authority (Homans, 1961). Persons find it difficult to comply with initiatives that they consider unfair.

Modern organizations normally make a further distinction within the vertical system of authority—the distinction between "line" and "staff" authority. The first is defined as general authority connected with overall supervision of a specific unit, such as a school system, a school, a department, or a classroom. Staff authority, on the other hand, is segmental and usually refers to some specialized aspect of the whole, as in the case of a central-office specialist working with teachers in several schools. There are strong arguments for creating and maintaining these two systems, which are found in almost all organizations above a given size. Yet it has been established that conflict is endemic to attempts to sustain two kinds of authority in the same organization; staff personnel complain, over and over again, of the unresponsiveness and limited knowledge of line supervisors while the latter charge specialists with excessive zeal and narrowness of outlook. Those familiar with schools have probably seen such tensions between elementary principals and central-office supervisors or high school teachers and counselors. The central point is that such difficulties are *not* unique to schools; they flow from the effort to differentiate between the authority of unit responsibility and the authority of specialized competence.

Students of organizations have learned that formal statements of authority and official definitions of working relationships (as in organization charts) are rarely, if ever, fully adequate descriptions of the day-to-day reality of organizational life. Departures from the formal are the rule rather than the exception. One of the early and signal studies of this matter was done by Roethlisberger and Dickson (1939), who found that factory workers had beliefs and ways of acting that differed sharply from management's; the workers, moreover, paced their production in light of *their* viewpoints. Dalton (1959) later provided us with a superb account of how formal prescription and actual behavior differ among industrial workers. School researchers, aware of such studies, looked for similar phenomena in schools and found them. Both Gordon (1957) and Cusick (1973) uncovered rich and complicated peer relationships and special norms among students that are, in fact, barely visible even to adults who work in schools. McPherson (1972) described informal relationships among teachers.

I hope the point that organizations of different kinds share important attributes has been sufficiently illustrated; a complete discussion would take more space than we have here. It seems clear that given the available evidence, it would be unwise for us to argue schools are entirely different from all other organizations—the similarities are too evident.

Schools, however, are more like some organizations than others, and we can trace similarities—and differences—by identifying school characteristics that place them in particular organizational categories. The similarity/difference anomaly is highlighted by such classification, for although schools share important attributes with some other organizations, they are not exactly similar. When we add up the similarities and differences, moreover, we find that no other organization features quite the same combination of characteristics.

Although obvious, it is nonetheless important that schools are *public* institutions. Financed through taxation, they are supposed to be responsive to the will of the electorate, a characteristic that Bailyn (1960) showed to have developed early in the history of American schools. In colonial New England, the basic arrangement of having local schools supervised by a group of leading citizens had already taken shape and is a feature that remains today (Cremin, 1970). The school board was composed of leading citizens who were to represent not only householders using schools, but the community at large, and the system of financial support that emerged—reliance on local property taxes—taxed all who possessed property. (Today we are, of course, moving to greater reliance on state support and as a consequence, to reliance on sales and income revenues as well as property taxes.) The public, tax-supported nature of schools makes them similar in important ways to fire and police departments, municipal and state universities, and other public services. It also differentiates them from most American organizations.

The consequences of public support become more apparent when we compare schools with private ventures. Businesses and private hospitals, for example, set prices for their goods and services that, given certain conditions, produce revenues exceeding expenses. The excess makes it possible for such ventures to accumulate additional resources and to assign them to whatever purposes the organizational leadership chooses, including expansion of services, addition of capital resources, and in profit-making enterprises, profits for the owners. Private ventures have, in essence, a high degree of organizational autonomy, for they need not "go to the public" to authorize particular plans or expenditures. School systems, on the other hand, are continuously dependent on the willingness of citizens to pay taxes and to support particular boards of education in their stated plans. In some cases, such as a capital undertaking, special elections must be held. Expenditures are sensitive to local political sentiment; it is a truism that angry citizens are not likely to support higher levels of expenditure.

Public schools face a further complication that is not found in most private undertakings. Take, for example, a furniture-manufacturing company. It typically must purchase lumber and contract for other costs before selling its product, normally going to banks and other benefactors for loans to do so. It sells its furniture to other parties; in short, its "input" and "output" problems are solved in different locations and with different people. Schools, however, are confronted with overlap in their input and output processes, in getting funds and "selling" their products—that is, in gaining acceptance for their performance. They must convince the local public, a large proportion of whom they serve directly, to support them financially; thus, difficulties at one end, so to speak, may be reflected at the other. Difficulties in school may dampen community support while low levels of support may in turn create difficulties in providing school services. Schools are "bound in" to their publics in a particularly intense way.*

The dependence of schools on local favor affects their capacity to set and achieve instructional goals. Their leaders are engaged in activities that we call "political," for lack of a more specific term. Because action taken within schools may influence the system's ability to develop support, administrators become sensitive to the community repercussions of school events. Programs may be inaugurated because they appeal to important subpublics; other actions may be vetoed lest they offend powerful groups or individuals who can influence resource allocation. Prudence is further institutionalized in the standard arrangement that makes the superintendent "vulnerable": He or she is normally employed under a short-term contract. [It is clear that superintendents see themselves as vulnerable to community pressures; research by Callahan (1962) and Gross, Mason, and McEachern (1958) documents the point.] Conflicts may arise within school systems, then, as teachers press for action that administrators deem unwise or as administrators make requests that teachers find unsuitable. Developing and sustaining clear instructional policies may become very difficult when the political environment is turbulent.

There is another consequence of the schools' dependence on public support. Because government budgets are short-run, usually based on an annual cycle, school planning is foreshortened. Long-range plans to raise performance to a given level or to develop complex programs are often ruled out. Plans are also subject to sudden reversal with changes in board membership or the departure of key administrators. This may explain, in part, why so many school innovations are faddish in nature and why we get a rapid succession of novelties and teacher cynicism about innovation. (Innovations, in fact, may be supported by federal agencies and foundations that impose short schedules of their own.) To sum up, the public nature of schooling imposes con-

---

* Although we cannot delve into it here, there is another important aspect of the school's public nature. Unlike private ventures, schools do not go out of business. Under law, schools must be available to the relevant population. This assurance of continuity undoubtedly has important effects on the workings of schools.

25

straints that are not present when organizations have sufficient financial autonomy to select and follow a steady course of action.

Schools belong to another limited set of organizations, those that deal with persons rather than things. They provide services, but those services are of a special kind. It is expected that successive provision of the services will produce changes in those receiving them. Some sociologists describe such services as "people work." All service organizations must be aware of their relationships with customers or clients, but in the case of schools and some others, the relationship is particularly intense, for it requires continuing cooperation and mutual confidence. This requires special efforts to incorporate into the organization the persons who are served; students are, in many ways, as much a part of the school as staff members are.

Schools, like other organizations of their kind, face a special dilemma in this matter of incorporating those who are served, particularly because the numbers involved are large and budgets are normally constricting. Large numbers require standardized treatment, the development and application of rules, and other bureaucratic procedures. Tension can arise between those routines and the preferences of students, and if tension runs high, it may undermine student confidence in the school and its staff. Waller (1932/1965) described the school as an organism in "perilous equilibrium" as students and teachers waged a kind of unremitting battle with each other. Although that description may apply to fewer schools today, the possibility always exists that organizational routines and controls will alienate students and inhibit effective teaching and learning.

The obvious fact that schools deal with children and adolescents has consequences that may be less obvious. One is that the identity of the clientele is confused. Another is that special problems are introduced in establishing and maintaining productive relationships between staff members and students.

Who are the clients of the school? At first glance, they are obviously the students. But students are legal minors whose parents are usually concerned with their children's fates and see themselves as legitimately involved in school events. Parents, then, are also clients, and in some cases, they can be influential in furthering or retarding community support for school programs. Because parents and their children do not always see eye to eye on what constitutes good schooling, the school may face a divided clientele. Schools are also preparatory institutions, shaping the young who will ultimately assume adult responsibilities. Thus, other interests are brought into play, and other groups see themselves as clients of the school. Employers seek suitable employees and press for what they consider appropriate curricula. The federal government becomes concerned about its needs for human resources, both military and civilian, and promotes particular programs related to those needs. Colleges set up entry standards that shape school activities while patriotic societies press to have specific values promulgated in the schools. These are but illustrations of the complex nature of the school's clientele and the tendency for that clientele to demand diverse, and sometimes conflicting, outcomes. Constructing and carrying out a school program is no simple matter and may require trade-offs of objectives to get acceptance. It may be difficult to concentrate resources to bring about clear-cut, mutually supportive objectives.

Experienced teachers are aware of the second consequence of dealing with children and adolescents, they are not yet mature. In some respects, teachers are trying to get regular work from irregular workers while teaching those who are still learning to learn. In other words, we can think of school professionals as making up the "deficit" in self-control, work motivation, learning skills, etc. among their students (Lortie, 1975). Because students are normally in groups, the particular immaturities of some children may force procedures on all that prove alienating; for example, to maintain order, teachers may be forced to become more austere than they wish to be. This tension between "discipline" and instilling confidence and enthusiasm among students is one of the fundamental issues of working with energetic young people. It is not faced in many organizations, and it uses up psychological resources that in other settings can be deployed in other ways.

Schools also belong to another class of organizations, those that use compulsion in bringing about participation. The American legal system forces all children of a given age to attend some school; teachers cannot assume that students are there as a consequence of their own free choice or even the choice of their parents. Our system of financial support, moreover, adds an additional element of compulsion because the attendance of students must be closely observed and controlled. The concepts of "average daily attendance" and compulsory attendance lead to an elaborate apparatus of registers, hall passes, medical excuses, and attendance officers. Teachers and school administrators take on, willy-nilly, some of the functions of prison guards, finding that much time is spent on noninstructional activities (Cusick, 1973). Research by Nault (1974) suggests that compulsion dampens involvement, for students who were free to choose their own schools showed considerably higher levels of engagement in school. One should not push the prison analogy too far; school professionals do considerably more than restrain individuals. But it is another facet of school organization that differentiates the school from most other formal organizations, and it affects aspects of the school's daily life.

We have found, then, that schools are both like and unlike other formal organizations and that awareness of the similarities can be useful to our understanding. Yet we cannot deny that schools have their special characteristics, which have important consequences. We have no alternative but to note the anomaly of simultaneous similarity and difference and live with it. To overlook the similarities is to cut ourselves off from a growing body of knowledge about organizations in general. But if we fail to take account of the unique properties of schools, we run the risk not only of incomplete and inaccurate knowledge, but also of denying the particular nature of education and its special mission in our society.

Anomaly Number 2: Complex But Simple

We can get some help in understanding the anomaly of simultaneous complexity and simplicity by tracing the development of American schools. For some of the confusion induced by the juxtaposition of a vast educational system and schools as collections of classrooms comes from exaggerating the similarities between schools and other kinds of organizations. We hear schools described as "big business" because they employ over two million persons and spend billions of dollars annually. Some writers use the rhetoric of organizational analysis without even indicating how schools differ from General Motors, the Roman Catholic Church, or the United States Marines. Our school history will necessarily be brief and incomplete, but should be understood as intended simply to elicit few special characteristics of schools.

Crucial components of our modern school system developed very early in our history. School boards, teachers, and students were present in 18th-century colonial America. The earliest school "committees" (they were originally subcommittees of local government) raised funds, built and repaired the schoolhouse, and hired the teacher. One teacher worked with all children—of whatever age—who were sent to school. Localism in school affairs got an early start and persisted after the formation of the Republic, for state governments were for many decades physically remote and politically weak.

Although school arrangements varied somewhat from place to place and time to time, the usual school came close to the early New England model well into the 19th century. The first multiple-classroom school was begun in Boston early in the 19th century. As cities grew, such schools flourished. The office of the principal emerged, and gradually, schools became collections of classes graded by age and student knowledge. Additional complexity soon followed as cities collected these schools into systems and placed a superintendent in charge of all the schools. The progression was from a school run by a single teacher, to a school made up of a few classrooms and teachers, to city systems with perhaps tens of thousands of such classrooms under a hierarchy headed by a superintendent. Today we may find additional intervening layers (associate and assistant superintendents, assistant principals, department heads, etc.), but the basic structure that developed in the second half of the 19th century remains.

There is an extremely important feature to notice in this organizational development: The basic building block of schools and school systems has been the single classroom in which one teacher works with a group of students. Growth has been "cellular" through the addition and

28

limited specialization of such units. The units have been graded, and in secondary schools, they have been further subdivided by subject, but throughout the entire period, schools and school systems have assigned particular students to particular teachers in the expectation that they would be together for an academic year at a time. In elementary schools today, the teacher normally teaches all major subjects to a given group; in secondary schools, each teacher is responsible for teaching a given subject or subjects to several groups.

Why mention such evident qualities of schools? The answer lies in observing that their growth has been fundamentally different from that of industry: Technical processes in schools have not followed the same course. There are some similarities, of course; for example, administrative units have become larger, the amounts of money have grown, and the administrative hierarchy has lengthened. But if we examine the development of industry, we find that it has developed through technology coupled with intense specialization, resulting in ever-increasing interdependence among those employed. Machine and automated technologies have produced "smaller" jobs, and because each job has involved a more limited set of tasks, the connections between it and others have intensified. By comparison, the role of the classroom teacher today is general rather than specialized. Furthermore, unlike persons working in industrial settings, teachers perform a large proportion of their basic tasks without interacting with other adults; the cellular structure of schools means limited rather than intensive interdependence. And, of course, there has been in education no equivalent to industrial gains in productivity; teachers must still spend many hours with students to obtain results. Teaching, in the lingo of economists, remains "labor intensive."

The enormous apparatus that has developed around education is certainly important in its own right; today schooling is considerably less local in outlook than it once was. Social changes account for much of this; communication, travel, and growing interconnections between governments and other agencies have moved us toward a national culture of education (Campbell, Cunningham, McPhee & Nystrand, 1970). But to describe the vast superstructure of education as a single headquarters directing a vast, interconnected corporation would be a mistake; it sits, rather, over an array of school districts and schools still marked by internal independence rather than close interdependence. Its influence is undoubtedly genuine, for it generates funds, ideas, and political pressures although some of these efforts, representing divergent points of view, may cancel each other out. We need considerable research, in fact, to understand better how this plethora of organized efforts actually influences classroom instruction.

We can now restate the anomaly in at least slightly clearer terms. Education does feature an enormous and complicated array of governmental and nongovernmental groups seeking to shape it. But the core activities of schools—day-in, day-out learning—occur in individual classrooms monitored by individual teachers working for long stretches of time in isolation from each other and without close surveillance by administrative superordinates. Schools are still composed of influential, somewhat isolated subunits called classrooms, and technical processes of instruction continue to be dominated by lectures, discussion, demonstrations, etc., as they have been for many decades. As yet, technical changes have not rearranged instruction into anything like the interdependence that we find in factories and other work places marked by high technology. Schools can be seen as federations of effort rather than as closely controlled mechanisms responding to central management and engineeringlike manipulation. Compared to other systems of work, schools still provide considerable occasion for the exercise of personal discretion by classroom teachers.

THREE PERSPECTIVES

Comparison, as we have seen, helps us to place what we are studying in a broader context, pointing out special characteristics and drawing attention to features that we might otherwise miss. In this section, we will undertake a focused comparison using three aspects of organizations that have received considerable attention. The reader will find that these specifics are less exotic than they may sound at first; they refer to facets of organizational life with which we are familiar in our everyday lives.

Bureaucratization, or, the Prevalence of Rules

Most of us, from time to time, get the urge to use the term "bureaucrat" as an expletive, particularly when we run up against some official who seems determined to obstruct our needs with some petty rule. However, the term also has a technical, less-heated meaning, originally developed by Max Weber, the giant of social science in Germany at the turn of the century (Gerth & Mills, 1946). Weber was interested in the sweep of human history and in the kinds of authority revealed there; to him bureaucratic authority was a distinct and relatively efficient form, observably different from the charisma of outstanding figures or the traditional authority of kings and others like them. Today, in just about every modern organization, we find to some extent the characteristics that he associated with bureaucracy.* But we also know, on the basis of everyday experience, that some organizations are "more bureaucratic"

---

* Weber's concept of bureaucracy included several components. There is a division of labor that permits specialization and expertness. The authority structure is hierarchical. Official actions and decisions are governed by a system of rules and regulations. Officials are expected to be impersonal in their relationships because personal feelings are likely to be the source of irrationality. There is a career system for officials that features hiring on the basis of attested competence, appointment rather than election, and payment by salary.

than others. For example, we implicitly recognize the difference between the intricate, massive rule system under which the Internal Revenue Service operates and the free-wheeling atmosphere of an avant garde art school. The latter may be run in ways that meet minimal criteria of bureaucracies, but no one would mistake it for a branch office of the tax collector. We find it useful, in short, to think of bureaucracy as a matter of degree, as a continuum on which we place different kinds of organizations or different organizations of the same type. (One army unit, for example, may be appreciably more bureaucratic than another.)

Bidwell, in a much-quoted article on school organization (1965), argued that schools meet the minimal criteria for a bureaucracy, but are toward the lower end of the bureaucratic spectrum; they are marked, he said, by "structural looseness." He accounted for this looseness by pointing to the tension between bureaucratic behavior as impersonal and distant, and the requirements in teaching for quite opposite kinds of behavior—warmth, empathy, attention to the individual child, etc. What is needed in teaching, in short, is not what is called for when a government agency deals with members of the public; the classification of each event and the application of a preselected rule are not suited to relationships with students. Too much emphasis on bureaucratic forms would reduce the school's capacity to meet its particular goals.

Lortie (1969) saw schools as applying different kinds of rules to different aspects of their organizations, arguing that while some activities are highly bureaucratized, others are not. For example, procedures for spending and accounting for funds are in the zone where "hard rules" apply; everyone involved is expected to conform to highly specific rules and can expect literal and forceful supervision in such matters. In other areas, however, there are "soft rules" and gentle enforcement. The language related to curriculum, for example, may be permissive, vague, and suggestive rather than mandatory, specific, and directive; people may speak of "outlines" and "alternative possibilities" rather than detailed instructions on how to fill out form 348-B. It is interesting, in fact, that the central commitment of schools—the provision of instruction—is generally less rule bound than more peripheral functions; thus, the same individual administrator may be directive in some matters, permissive in others. The sensibilities of teachers, moreover, seem to coincide with these zones; the same teacher who would resent any "interference" in his or her classroom work may criticize the principal for being too lax in making sure that other teachers do their share of hall duty.

Recent work by Hanson (1973) has built on this earlier view of partial bureaucratization in schools. After close-in study of California schools, Hanson developed "the interacting spheres model" to account for relationships between teachers and administrators. Teachers and administrators are depicted as occupying different spheres of influence, with different kinds of decisions delegated to each party. Administrators for example, may hold clear title to decisions concerned with security, the allocation of resources, boundary matters (such as relationships be-tween the school and the community), and evaluation, but teachers claim instructional decisions as their domain. Both parties engage in various types of maneuvers to defend their terrain and to find resolutions for issues that have no obvious location. Hanson believes that the bureau-cratic model is poorly suited to situations where professionals are super-vised, for it makes too little provision for the judgment and discretion exercised by persons in professional work.

Much research remains to be done on bureaucratization in schools, both in terms of their position relative to other systems and the variations (and consequences of such variations) between different schools and school systems. At this point, however, it is possible to say that schools are not at the extremes of the continuum. For example, Kaufman (1960) described how the ranger's work is controlled by hundreds and hundreds of regulations that are regularly updated. No teacher or principal con-fronts a rule book of the kind encountered by the forest ranger. But neither are teachers and principals completely free of rules and specifications laid down by the state government, the school board, and others; their work is considerably more regulated, for example, than that of physicians in a clinic or professors in a private institution. Rules play a large enough part in the daily life of schools to receive close attention from those who would understand them better and from those who would like to see them operate more effectively. This is particularly important since greater state participation in financial support may lead to greater bureaucratization of schools in general (Lortie, 1975).

Professionals in Organizations

The classical model of bureaucracy does not deal with the fact that in some settings, subordinates who do the core tasks of the organization define themselves as professionals with special competence and par-ticular rights to autonomy. Technical work may be done by persons with few skills and little training, as in factories hiring unskilled or semiskilled workers. It may, on the other hand, require special skills and protracted preparation. Organizations are pressed to adjust to the characteristics of those performing core tasks, be they insurance clerks, welders, surgeons, or salespersons. How do teachers fare in this regard? Specifically, how do their prerogatives compare with those at the ex-tremes of high professionalization and no professionalization at all?

We will compare technical personnel in different settings, using three sets of criteria found in the literature on organizations. One is the scope of the discretion allowed to the technical person—over how wide a range is the person expected to make his or her own decisions? Second, how often is the subordinate's work reviewed, and what are the consequences of a negative evaluation? Third, we will inquire into the positive powers possessed by the professional group; how much formal authority does the colleague group have in operating the organization?

The worker on the assembly line has an extremely low level of personal discretion. He or she must comply, in great detail, with operations designed by management, closely supervised by superiors, and paced by workings of the machine system. At the other extreme, the surgeon in a hospital is expected to make decisions about the course of treatment without direction from administrative superordinates. In the middle ranges, we find news reporters, beat police officers, and nurses making decisions, but doing so within clearly established limits and under the close supervision of organizational superiors.

The discretionary scope of the individual teacher varies with experience (especially with tenured versus nontenured status), specialty, and local reputation; persons who have demonstrated competence through time or who possess scarce, specialized knowledge normally receive less supervision than others. Teacher discretion in general is a mixed case, being broad in some respects and narrow in others. Teachers usually have considerable autonomy in handling the interpersonal aspects of teaching. Although there is normally a local definition of what constitutes an acceptable level of discipline, teachers handle specifics such as timing, pacing, and the myriad details of classroom management—areas of autonomy that receive support because of their physical isolation and because of informal norms inhibiting intervention in classroom affairs by administrators. Yet teachers are normally expected to work within the confines of a predesignated curriculum that places limits on what they will teach; individual teachers in most schools (with exceptions in experimental settings) have little say on general content. Moreover, local situations have their local taboos, which teachers soon encounter, and it seems that when teachers violate such taboos, their power to offset recrimination is low. (We could use research on how such taboos and their effects are changing under circumstances of collective bargaining and altered lifestyles.)

In contrast to others in the middle ranges, teacher work is reviewed at relatively infrequent intervals, a fact that points to greater autonomy; and review is normally not as threatening to teachers as it is to those in the other fields. The reporter's work is visible to superordinates on a daily basis, and superordinates may, in fact, alter the reporter's stories before publication. The police officer works in a military-like system, clearly under orders and surveillance from superior officers; his or her actions can be reviewed at any time. The nurse works under the direction of senior nurses and physicians who feel no compunction about noting mistakes and taking action. Beginning teachers are reviewed annually, and decisions about retention or nonretention are made for that period of time, but the most striking difference between teachers and others lies in the reduction in personal threat associated with tenure arrangements. One must be careful, of course, not to exaggerate the vulnerability of others—for example, police officers are usually protected by civil service rules, and informal norms proscribe the arbitrary firing of news reporters or nurses—but teachers can count on continued employment to a considerably greater extent than most salaried employees can. Economic security reduces the danger posed by superordinate review and bolsters autonomy. Also, because the largest single category of teachers working today is constituted of married women, few of whom aspire to administrative positions, superordinate influence over personal goals is further reduced.

The relatively broad scope of discretion and the comparatively infrequent and lower threat of review are not, however, matched by corresponding positive powers for the teacher group. In this regard, teachers do not possess the equivalent power, for example, of professors in major universities or physicians in hospitals, nor do they noticeably surpass others in the middle ranges. Teachers may, of course, serve on committees dealing with wider school matters, but although their influence may not be negligible under such circumstances, it remains essentially advisory. In formal terms, teachers are not part of the governance structure of the public schools. All such formal powers rest with the school board, and in some jurisdictions, specific rights are also ascribed to the superintendent. Collective bargaining contracts may put limits on what school administrators may require of teachers in terms of effort, time, etc., but they rarely increase the joint capacity of teachers to initiate activity within the school system (Perry & Wildman, 1970). Professors, by contrast, not only determine the content of the courses that they teach, but they collectively (through departments, senates, etc.) shape their institutions. Professors also play a major part in deciding who joins the faculty and their subsequent fates. Similar powers are exercised by medical staffs in hospitals. The assertiveness of teachers has centered on limiting the ability of superordinates to influence their work and personal interests; it has done relatively little to make teachers a professional force in the governance of schools and school systems.

Seen as professionals in organizations, then, teachers are anomalous. They have comparatively high discretion in matters of method, high job security, and freedom from incessant review. As a collegial group, however, they exercise no appreciably greater power than those in other middle-range occupations such as news reporting, nursing, or police work and less than those in academics and medicine. Although teachers have built certain protections through their associations and unions, they do not exercise shared authority over instructional or personnel matters, and the individual teacher has limited ability to shape his or her own daily work. Teachers must practice their craft, in fact, in settings where others hold general hegemony; they cannot be sure that superordinates will make all possible efforts to facilitate their work and help them earn their psychic rewards (Lortie, 1975). In many respects, teachers remain dependent on the good will of administrative superiors and parents; their freedom from intervention exceeds their freedom to arrange their work as they think best.

On Technology

The word technology conjures up images of interlocking gears, bubbling beakers, and throbbing motors, but we can also use it broadly to refer to the activities and know-how connected with the basic tasks of an organization. The term combines two related sets of ideas: the ways in which work is processed, and knowledge of cause-and-effect relationships underlying that processing. In the first sense, that of work-flow, we can readily identify the technological styles of schools; as far as the second is concerned, school technological knowledge suffers from general weaknesses in our knowledge of human behavior and our lack of a scientific pedagogy.

Thompson (1967) presents a threefold scheme of technology that can help us examine the case of schools. One type is mediating technology, in which work-flows center on bringing persons together and satisfying their diverse needs, as in a bank where borrowers and savers pool their requirements. The second type consists of long-linked technologies, which emphasize the need to perform steps in a particular order; automobile assembly is an excellent example. Standardization of procedure plays an important part in both mediating and long-linked technologies. In assembly-line production, standardizing the product maximizes control and permits those managing it to iron out difficulties with experience; in mediating technologies, the needs of participating parties are processed through a common set of standards, as in a bank where bookkeeping is routinized and categories are set up for designating different types of loans. Thompson's third type, intensive technology, does *not* rely on standardization, for in this type the emphasis is on the individual project or the individual. Work processes are organized around the particular needs of the individual case, and work is paced by feedback about it. A general hospital epitomizes intensive technology; the treatment of each patient (for example, bringing specific resources to bear on his or her illness) is supposed to occur as the condition dictates.

School technology is illuminated by Thompson's categories. School technology is partly mediating, for it brings teachers and students together. Even Illich (1971), who would do away with schools, found it necessary to suggest alternative mechanisms for bringing would-be learners together with those having the knowledge to teach them. Schools are also long linked, for sequence is the essence of grading and is integral to the progression of learning in some subjects. Schools are occasionally intensive, as when they or individual teachers can provide for the special needs of individual students. Their regular modes of operation, however, involve "batching" students into classes and moving them through a predesigned set of learning experiences. Perhaps

35

because they have stressed mediating and long-linked technologies, schools have relied heavily on standardization procedures such as standard grading, standard curricula, fixed policies for admission, promotion, and graduation, required subjects, etc.

Current trends and auguries of change seem particularly relevant in this matter of school technology. Many of the pressures now playing on schools—and ideals of a future desirable state for them—posit considerable shift in regular modes of operation. Cellular structure and standardization are challenged by innovations that stress greater team-work among professionals and greater individualization in instruction. Critics who attack schools as "lockstep" or "inhumane" or "not diverse enough" reject past criteria based on the presumed desirability of uniformity and standardization. Implicitly or explicitly, they are calling for schools with more complex and sensitive repertoires of experiences for students. We can see a similar shift when those administering reading programs talk of "prescribing" particular mixes of teaching content and methods for individual students or when experimental projects are designed to "tailor" programs to the needs of students. When public schools offer alternative programs and announce that they do so because different children benefit from different approaches, they are moving toward intensive technology and deserting earlier ideals of standardization. All of this takes place in a time when bicultural education, special efforts to help minorites play a greater role in schools, and other programs emplhasizing cultural pluralism further erode the notion of the "one best system" (Tyack, 1974).

We must exercise caution in projecting the future from current emphases: How does one measure the strength and staying power of any given theme when fads move in and out? Yet those involved in schools might be advised to watch such movements away from the work processes and assumptions of the past; it may not be long before teachers and administrators find themselves constructing a new school technology that is complicated and difficult to operate. Whatever form it takes, it will in all probability require considerably more interaction among professionals and feature considerably more organizational complexity than we have heretofore seen in public schools.

SOME CONCLUDING COMMENTS

The system of schooling that we have examined in the preceding pages was developed during the 19th century and elaborated in the 20th. The first task, one of enormous magnitude, was to create schools that would be available to all young Americans. It is one of the achievements of American society that it constructed the first system of mass, free schooling. That system was built according to organizational ideas available at the time and in terms of values that were paramount then:

Schools were to follow hierarchical principles and stress uniformity in procedure; equality of treatment would flow from carefully administered, bureaucratic arrangements. Teachers were subordinated at the end of a long ladder of authority, but protections were developed over the years, such as tenure, payment by seniority and education, and later, collective-bargaining agreements. Although informal norms developed to soften the impact of hierarchical authority, official powers remained at the apex of the pyramid, and few explicit powers of governance were granted to teachers. Joining with other pressures in the same direction, the system encouraged teachers to "privatize" their work (Lortie, 1975). Teachers came to focus their concerns and energies on classroom affairs, leaving other matters to administrators and to others interested in "educational politics."

Teachers' lack of concern about the broader context of schooling may, however, be less desirable today—a possibility that I mentioned at the outset of this paper. Shifts in school finance, for example, are placing increasing powers in the hands of state officials who operate at a distance from local schools. Will they honor informal restraints on authority practiced by local school officials? Or will the increase in state participation result in a more bureaucratic system in which teachers and administrators are pressed into a civil service mold?

The research-and-development frame of mind, coupled with trends toward more individualization of instruction, may lead to important changes in instructional programs. Parents, for example, may demand more choices for their children; such demands might lead to voucher systems, more alternative schools, or some as-yet-not-visible approach stressing less standardization and greater attention to individual needs and/or preferences. What are currently experiments in technical intensity may prove attractive and spread. If so, new structures, featuring teamwork among professionals, will emerge. The image of instruction as primarily a relationship between an individual teacher and a group of students may give way to complex new patterns that combine diverse resources of personnel and varieties of new techniques. Teachers who define instruction solely as that which occurs within their own classrooms may find themselves lords of a shrinking domain.

Teachers who wish to retain and increase their influence over instruction would be wise to increase their awareness of the context of schooling. They should keep abreast of new developments and join with colleagues in exploring, testing, and assessing novel approaches and claims coming from various innovators. Collegial action will require closer working relationships with peers, and effectiveness in joint activities will be increased to the extent that teachers are familiar with the intricacies of their work settings.

REFERENCES

Bagehot, W. *Physics and Politics*. New York: Knopf, 1948.
Bailyn, B. *Education in the Forming of American Society*. Chapel Hill: N.C.: University of North Carolina Press, 1960.
Barnard, C. *The Functions of the Executive*. Cambridge, Mass.: Harvard University Press, 1938.
Bidwell, C. "The School as a Formal Organization." In J. G. March, ed. *The Handbook of Organizations*. Chicago: Rand McNally, 1965, pp. 972-1022.
Campbell, R., Cunningham, L. L., McPhee, R., and Nystrand, O. *The Organization and Control of American Schools*. Columbus, Ohio: Merrill, 1970.
Callahan, R. E. *Education and the Cult of Efficiency*. Chicago, Ill.: University of Chicago Press, 1962.
Cremin, L. A. *American Education: The Colonial Experience. 1607-1783*. New York: Harper & Row, 1970.
Cusick, P. A. *Inside High School*. New York: Holt, Rinehart and Winston, 1973.
Dalton, M. *Men Who Manage*. New York: Wiley, 1959.
Gerth, H., and Mills, C. W., trans. and eds. *From Max Weber: Essays in Sociology*. Glencoe, Ill.: Free Press, 1946.
Gordon, C. W. *The Social System of the High School*. Glencoe, Ill.: Free Press, 1957.
Gross, N., Mason, W. S., and McEachern, A. W. *Explorations in Role Analysis: Studies of the School Superintendency Role*. New York: Wiley, 1958.
Hanson, M. "The Emerging Control Structure of the Schools," *Administrator's Notebook* 21 (1973): 2. (Newsletter from Midwest Administration Center, 5835 Kimbark Ave., Chicago, Ill. 60637.)
Homans, G. *Social Behavior: Its Elementary Forms*. New York: Harcourt, Brace and World, 1961.
Illich, I. *Deschooling Society*. New York: Harper & Row, 1971.
Kaufman, H. *The Forest Ranger: A Study in Administrative Behavior*. Baltimore, Md.: Johns Hopkins Press, 1960.
Lortie, D. C. "The Balance of Control and Autonomy in Elementary School Teaching." In *The Semi-Professions and Their Organization*, A. Etzioni, ed. New York: Free Press, 1969, pp. 1-53.
Lortie, D. C. *Schoolteacher: A Sociological Study*. Chicago, Ill.: University of Chicago Press, 1975.
McPherson, G. *Small Town Teacher*. Cambridge, Mass.: Harvard University Press, 1972.
Nault, R. "School Affiliation and Student Commitments: A Study of the Initial School Commitments of Nonpublic School Freshmen Voluntarily and Involuntarily Affiliated with their Schools." Unpublished doctoral dissertation, University of Chicago, 1974.
Perry, C. R., and Wildman, W. A. *The Impact of Negotiations on Public Education: The Evidence from the Schools*. Worthington, Ohio: Charles A. Jones, 1970.
Roethlisberger, F., and Dickson, W. J. *Management and the Worker*. Cambridge, Mass.: Harvard University Press, 1939.
Thompson, J. D. *Organizations in Action*. New York: McGraw-Hill, 1967.
Tyack, D. *The One Best System: A History of American Urban Education*. Cambridge, Mass.: Harvard University Press, 1974.
Waller, W. *The Sociology of Teaching*. New York: Wiley, 1965. (Originally published by Russell and Russell, 1932.)

Section 2: Schools as Social Organizations

Melvin M. Tumin

A distinctive feature of all modern industrial societies is the fact that a majority of both the adult and child populations spend most of their energetic waking hours inside large scale organizations. For the adults this means at their places of work; for the children, this means at their schools. The individual offices, plants or schools where these hours are spent may be relatively small compared to the larger organizations of which they are members, and some of the impact of largeness may thereby be reduced. But there can be little doubt that large overall organizations are dominant and influential environments in the lives of all who live and work in them.

It is also characteristic of modern industrial societies that the influences of these environments of large scale organizational life are democratically distributed, in the sense that they commonly affect those who sit at the top of the ladder of occupational prestige and income, (such as professionals, managers and directors of large corporate enterprises), those in the middle of the ladder (such as teachers), and those at the bottom rungs of the ladder (such as unskilled manual laborers). In sum, the influences of membership in large organizations are a common, shared fact of life.

THE CASE AGAINST TECHNOLOGICAL SOCIETY

Yet, the terms in which those democratically spread large organizations are frequently characterized are such as to make them appear not only totally undesirable but indeed unnecessary and avoidable abominations.

Thus, such organizations are commonly described, often with much adverse feeling, as bureaucratic, impersonal, cold, heartless, inhumane, machine-like and alienating. Moreover, they are often seen as the deliberate creations of inhumane and profit-crazy entrepreneurs and power-hungry bureaucrats, and it is alleged that such people have deliberately chosen this monstrous model of organization to inflict on the powerless masses of mankind in preference to a number of alternative organizational models that would be far more positively resonant with the best of the human spirit and far more mindful and conserving of valuable qualities of mankind.

Similar terms and ideas are commonly used, as well, to denounce technological industrial society in general. Here the accusation is that machines have gotten the best of their human creators; that these machines have acquired an autonomy of their own; that they dominate humans; and that in the process they deplete the human spirit of its richness, human life of its vitality, and human society of its humanity. Here too it is asserted that technological society is not necessary; that it is an evil of which we can rid ourselves; and that we are afflicted by it only because enemies of humanity deliberately employ machines on behalf of profits, in utter disregard of all other human values.

This antitechnological, antiorganizational point of view is often most eloquently and heatedly expounded on college campuses. Nor is it surprising that college youth should adopt this critical posture. For they constitute the segment of the population that is perhaps freest of the deplored influences of modern industrial life. Moreover, they have a continuous exposure, in their courses and readings, to a variety of viewpoints, both historical and contemporaneous, from which to criticize life in modern society; and they have the leisure and luxury, more than almost anyone else, to read and think about and debate alternative life styles. Frequently, too, they are formally rewarded in their courses, and informally by their peers, for imaginative envisioning of such alternative life styles, especially those that might reduce the undesirable impacts of large scale organizational environments and that might even conceivably be implemented.

Doubtless, too, the critical stance of college students is partly attributable to the bitter realization by the college students that a majority of them will at some time in the proximate future be required, if they are to make their livelihoods, to join the rest of the adult world in large organizational environments. That being their predictable future, it is surely of the utmost importance that they should come to understand the structure and functioning of such organizations, all the more so if they intend either to try to ward off the feared dehumanizing influences, or, even more adventurously, to alter those environments so that their impacts may be more humane. Such an understanding can be greatly useful, of course, to those about to enter the teaching profession. For school systems are good examples of large scale organizations and share many common features with all other such organizations, however much they may differ in other regards.

SOME USEFUL POSITIVE PERSPECTIVES ON TECHNOLOGY, GROWTH AND ORGANIZATION

Some general perspectives about industrial society and large scale organizations may prove useful in coming to terms with the problems in front of us.

They are Impersonal, Natural Developments

First, it is crucial that these features of modern life be seen as impersonal, historical, understandable occurrences that arise quite naturally, and without plotting or conspiracy, in the course of societal growth and expansion. This view contrasts sharply of course with that which holds that industrialization and large scale organization have been maliciously and deliberately foisted on a powerless and gullible population. Now, to see these developments as natural, impersonal social processes is not to affirm the desirability of growth, but only to note that the dynamic of growth has been a central feature of industrialization since its onset. If therefore a "no growth" or "zero growth" theme seems now to be commanding greater public attention, this has to be understood as a reaction to the "growth-is-good" theme that has dominated modern industrial life for more than 200 years.

They Have Brought Many Benefits

Second, however much certain special small groups of people may have benefitted disproportionately from the growth of societies and of organizations within them, there can be little doubt that many important and widely shared values have also been served by these growth features. Health has been improved; longevity increased and more democratically distributed; infant mortality cut down sharply; real income significantly improved; desired consumption goods made widely available; democratic government reinforced; educational opportunities extended beyond anyone's earlier imaginings; immigrant populations far more easily incorporated into various societies than would otherwise ever have been possible; illiteracy virtually exterminated; fast and cheap communication and transportation, and entertainment and diversion of the greatest variety made available to masses of people.

I need not recite the counterbalancing negative values of pollution, and crowding, and mass wars of great destructive powers, and new forms of exploitation. Those are the well-known particulars of the bill of indictment against modern industrial society. Rather I list in some detail the gains that such growth has made possible so that it can be seen that growth and industrialization have not had unilaterally negative effects, but that, to the contrary, there has been a significant value tradeoff. The balance of desirable and undesirable outcomes of growth and large size has to be judged. But such judgment will be neither well informed nor helpful if the mixed value outcomes in the tradeoff are not recognized.

These Benefits Could Not Otherwise Have Been Realized

Third, it can be shown that the valued outcomes recited above are in large part due to efficient organization of human and machine labor in large organizational networks. That is, the valued outcomes are not simply accidental or incidental to the industrial growth process. Rather, many if not most of them simply could not have been achieved without large scale industrialization and organization. Thus, without being able to specify exactly what are the sizes of critical masses of people that are needed, one can say confidently that substantial aggregates of people, living in fairly densely populated places which we call cities, are indispensable if one is to have museums, libraries, theatres, opera houses, concert halls, variegated shops and department stores, hospitals, universities, and well-equipped schools.

Above all, if large numbers of people are to be employed at decent wages they must be aggregated into common places of work; and if their productivity is to increase, so that there can be genuine increases in their real standards of living, then machine energy must increasingly be substituted for human energy. Someone has recently calculated that the amount of machine energy per capita in the United States today is equal to what could be supplied if each person had between 100 and 200 slaves. Some may think that a more desirable state of affairs. Needless to say, one would have to wonder what the slave population would consider desirable.

Given Today's Populations, There Are No Alternatives

Nor is it realistic to talk of numerous alternative trade-offs available to most of us. Unless one wants to talk of triage, i.e., choosing who is to live and who is to die, or, on a more modest scale, who is to enjoy life and who not, we have few if any alternatives to efficient large scale organization. One can test this out easily by asking oneself what one would do if one were in a city whose population included one million children of school age, 6-18, with perhaps 300,000 of them or more wanting to go on beyond a 12th year to some advanced education. How would one go about providing anything resembling education for those numbers? Idyllic dreams of small numbers of students engaged in unwalled educational exchanges with kindly proctors and mentors may be fine and even realizable for small numbers, but what do we do with a million young people all of whom, by any just theory of entitlement, are equally entitled to what our communities have to offer? How could we deschool them? Or train them outside the walls? How could we even achieve the bare literacy that deplorably is the most that a number of such children ever achieve, except in organized schools?

One might argue that one doesn't need high schools that contain two thousand students in one massive complex; that one could have much smaller units, perhaps like residential colleges, and perhaps that would be possible IF one could secure consent and support from taxpayers for the doubling, tripling, and quadrupling of school costs that such new ventures would unadvoidably entail. But that "if" ia a very large "if," and only the richest school districts in the country have managed to approximate any version of such decentralization. Gymnasiums, libraries, laboratories, playgrounds, auditoriums, heating and cooling plants, all of which are indispensable features of any good school, require large sums of money and any effort to provide them for numerous, small, decentralized, aggregates of students involves horrendous costs that most taxpayers are simply unwilling to bear. It is no accident, of course, that numbers of small school districts that commonly desire to provide their student residents with decent educational facilities have had to aggregate through regionalization to collectively afford that which none of them could afford on their own.

Without now pursuing other alternative schemes for the decentralization of educational organizations, I believe it can be firmly and correctly claimed that relatively large-size school organizations are the predictable environment of education in which most students and most teachers in this society will study and play and work in the future, assuming, that is, that we continue to value education for all, and continue to believe that all are equally entitled to as good schooling as is possible, and for as long as possible.

THREE MAJOR CHARACTERISTICS OF SCHOOL ORGANIZATION

We may now ask what are the characteristics of school organizations with which new teachers must learn to deal?

First we may specify three features which school systems share with all other large-scale formal organizations. There are: (1) bureaucratic organization; (2) hierarchical distribution of power and responsibility; (3) varied constituent memberships and formal structure.

Some of the implications of each of these three are worthy of being drawn out.

Bureaucratic Structure

While bureaucracy is often used as a dirty word, it is an indispensable term to characterize the structure that any organization of large numbers of people is virtually forced to assume if it is to operate with any degree of efficiency at all. The many tasks the organization has to perform have to be divided up and assigned to various bureaus and functionaries, with specific and explicit sets of responsibilities, and the correlative powers and rights they need to carry out their functions. Such organization of functions into bureaus, with delegated rights and responsibilities, provides orderliness, predictability and accountability. At least it makes those things far more possible than would otherwise be the case. It enables people to "count on" others; to know where to turn for help with various kinds of problems; to know with reasonable certainty that people will be at specified places at specified times, doing what they are supposed to be doing. Such organization makes it possible to determine the source of difficulties when things are not going well.

Whenever bureaucracies fail to function well, therefore, the fault lies not in the fact of a bureaucratic structure as such, but in the failure of its human members to perform according to prescription, schedule and expectation. Since human beings frequently do not perform according to expectations, the structures in which these expectations are embedded frequently do not function well.

When this is the case, then one must ask what is at fault: Are the expectations too high? Are the resources required for adequate job function adequate? Are the incentives and motivations for conscientious work sufficiently well developed? Are the functionaries adequately trained for their tasks? Have they been socialized into the ethic of conscientious work? Do they have adequate identification with the requirements and goals of the organization, or do they seek to maximize their individual advantages within the organization? Are superiors inflexible and lacking in understanding? Do the lines of communication function adequately? Do people know what they are supposed to do and why? And when? All of these are possible sources of the malfunctioning of bureaucratic structures.

Lest this inventory of possible malfunctions be seen as peculiar to bureaucracies, it should be noted that without such a formal structure of status, or positions, and roles, or sets of rights and responsibilities, matters would almost surely be intolerably worse. For the real breakdown of collective human effort occurs when the division of labor is unclear, when powers and rights are unspecified, when expectations are not set, and when there is no formal structure of accountability.

There is not adequate time here to go into the numerous studies of bureaucracies and their functioning to reveal the major types of understandings that have been developed. Suffice it to say that however much we may rebel against such formalized structures of collective work, no adequate substitute has ever been discovered. The model of communal, equal, spontaneous cooperation that so many romantically advocate can be thought of as a substitute only under three conditions, none of which can be said to be the least bit attainable in large-scale school systems. One condition is smallness of numbers of people involved so that everyone's actions are highly visible to everyone else. A second condition is the presence of a commonly shared deep concern of everyone involved for the well being of everyone else, and a common and equal sense of responsibility to the collective well being. The third condition is that everything that happens to the collective enterprise hurts or benefits all participants alike and is so perceived.

These conditions are realized, if at all, in small families, and then only after many years of happy, productive, satisfying collective life have been experienced, and during the course of which the major problems involved in group life have been worked out to the mutual satisfaction of everyone concerned. Needless to say, such happy, productive long-lasting small family groups are not very common, not even in the universe of families. So for better or for worse, whenever we attempt to "educate" large numbers of children under one common roof, or within the framework of one organizational structure, some bureaucratic organization of the school's functions is unavoidable.

No generalized prescription can be written to insure that such bureaucracies will work well or that they will be more humane, warm and personal than their structure suggests. But some key terms in this vein of thought, that is, of humanizing bureaucracies, are flexibility, patience, conscientiousness, allowance for human shortcomings, rotating turns at doing more than one's formal share of the burden and reciprocity. These attributes cannot be formally built into an organization; but the leadership of the bureaucracy can set a tone that makes it more or less likely that these attributes will be manifested throughout the organization. Above all, constant reiteration of the fact that the schools are for the education of children, and constant checking of programs and plans for their probable contribution to that education, may serve as salutary correctives on tendencies for the bureaucracies to act as if they were their own reason for being.

Hierarchy

Like bureaucracy, the term "hierarchy" is laden with negative connotations. An image is quickly evoked of pyramidal inequality and autocracy. Ordering, commanding, forbidding, prescribing: these are the modalities that are often associated with the term. But in fact the term in principle is neutral. All it literally implies is that there is inequality in power and in decision making. And such inequality is clearly neither good nor bad per se. It all depends, as always, on how the power is authorized and exercised.

The necessity of hierarchy is created by the presence of bureaucracy. There is no way for large numbers of people to be coordinated into an efficient organization without some approved mechanisms for deciding between competing ideas, conflicting interests and contrary values. Someone has to be given the responsibility, and hence held accountable, for the efficient functioning of the overall organization. Someone has to have the power to reward for a conscientious performance and to punish or otherwise restrain unwanted and disfunctional deviations from expectations. In sum, the need to decide, and often to decide quickly, among competing ideas, and the need to have the power to get people to conform to their role responsibilities demands a hierarchical structure of power.

This is not to say that all decisions always have to be referred to the top of the pyramid of power for decision. To the contrary: Some of the best functioning hierarchies are those in which significant percentages of decisions are delegated to autonomous or quasi-autonomous units lower down in the hierarchy. In schools this means department and division heads, curriculum coordinators, assistant principals, and teacher and student groups. So there are many possible shapes to hierarchies, and many possible different modes of functioning. But some hierarchy is indispensable for the coordination of the efforts of the many people involved in the bureaucratic structures.

Hierarchies, then, can and do vary on the tightness of their controls; the rigidity of role enforcement; the amount of scrutiny of performance; the competence of functionaries for their specialized positions; the fairness of the rewards and punishments; the amount of power that is delegated; the kinds and amounts of decisions in which people at all levels are allowed or encouraged to participate; the frequency with which decisions are reviewed and revised where need be; the openness of leaders or suggestions for change; the degree of consideration and understanding extended for human shortcomings. All those possible variations in hierarchical structures become key points to consider when one is asking how one can make the formal structure of work more agreeable, more productive, more invigorating, more humanly satisfying.

Multiple Constituents

Here we refer to the fact that the memberships of almost all organizations, and particularly school systems, are made up of numerous sets of actors or functionaries, each of which is certain to have rather different views as to what is important and what trivial, what is urgent and what can wait, what is worth lots of time and energy and what should command few scarce resources. Moreover because these different cohorts—students, teachers, administrators, service people and the like—come to the school system with different expectations and anticipations, they are also likely to disagree on what constitutes a successful day, week, or year in the life of the enterprise.

That amount of variability would be sufficiently perplexing and complex by itself. But one must add to that the further variability that one finds among teachers themselves, and students themselves, and among administrators and service people and members of boards of education. Only for some limited purposes can one deal with these major categories of organizational membership as uniform or homogeneous.

IMPLICATIONS: THE NATURALNESS OF CONFLICT. The implications here are numerous and important. First is the inevitability of conflict between the categories of members and within each of their own ranks. Conflict, like bureaucracy and hierarchy, sounds menacing and undesirable. But once again we use it as a neutral term to characterize the situation where values, goals, interests, and ideologies are in disagreement and where they come into confrontation with each other and hence must somehow be compromised or otherwise resolved.

We are saying the conflict is natural to school organizations, especially those in democratic societies; and most particularly in those democratic societies, such as ours, in which everyone involved feels expertly equipped to prescribe how education ought to be run, not excluding parents and students. If everyone involved has some entitlement to speak up—as they do—and if everyone feels fairly well versed in school theory and practice—as they do—and if everyone can exercise some influence on the decisions that are made—as they can—then we must expect schools to be natural combat zones. Nor is this to be deplored, at least not until one measures the educational outcomes of such conflictful educational environments against more monolithic, authoritarian structures of decision making and conflict resolution.

This is again not to say that conflict per se is good; but nor is it bad per se. It all depends on what is in conflict, what mechanisms are available for conflict resolution, and how much concern is commonly held by conflicting parties for certain common values and goals.

MODES OF DEMOCRATIC CONFLICT RESOLUTION. The general rule for decision making in a democracy is that everyone who will be affected by a decision should participate at his or her relevant level of competence. The key terms, of course, are "relevant level of competence". We may confidently expect much change in the years to come with regard to what is considered the relevant level of competence of students and teachers on various issues of school structure and functioning, because in the past these two groups have been traditionally excluded from participation in important decisions affecting their well being and that of the school in general. But new themes of democratic participation have come into vogue and these are not likely easily to vanish or die, however much they may modestly retreat from some recent excesses.

THE GROWTH OF COUNTERVAILING POWER BLOCS. In past years, conflicts were resolved by fiat from above and most often without any real contribution or participation by people at lower levels of the hierarchies of power. Now however, teachers have come increasingly to realize that the only possible way to muster power countervailing to that of the administrators and boards of education is to organize into power blocs. The single perhaps most significant change in school structure and functioning in the last several decades has been the adoption of the blue-collar model of trade union organization by the teachers. Formerly decried as unprofessional, such trade unions have come increasingly to the fore in recent years, and the traditionally softer local, state and national educational associations have had to become more militant, more willing to strike, more demanding rather than pleading to retain the loyalties and paid dues of their members. It can hardly be doubted that in the very proximate future there will be some effective merging of the AFL-CIO teachers' unions and the various branches of the NEA.

One may discover many negative features in school conduct that have emerged in the course of the growth of the trade union model. But if one does so, one must balance these against what the negatives were in the school situation and the condition of teachers before they became organized, and what their situations would be like today if they did not have collective power, through their organizations, to defend what they consider their legitimate rights and interests.

Predictably, we shall go through a rather messy and nasty decade or two of increasingly acerbic confrontation politics in school systems, as teachers' organizations seek to overcome what they consider the unjustified deficiencies in the teachers' situation. Moreover, one can confidently expect that school administrators will themselves become more organized and more militant.

Once again it is important to see these developments as natural occurrences, given the general ambience of the national culture and the special situations of the schools. Such teachers and administrators as unions are no more the malicious product of antieducational forces than were the traditional models of school governance that are now changing everywhere. We are simply moving from one model of school governance to another. Whether the net effect on the education of children in the schools is positive or negative is impossible to say. So many variables have to be considered when trying to account for what children learn or do not learn that one cannot with any good sense at all say that organized teacher power is responsible either for the gains or losses in the educational outcomes.

There is little doubt, for example, that lifetime tenure can easily lead to irresponsibility, laziness and sloth on the part of teachers. There is equally little doubt that being continuously subject to the arbitrary whimsical authority of administrators can easily lead to servile, deferential antieducational behavior on the part of teachers as well. So, the evil, if there is evil, lies not in tenure as such, but in its abuses. Since all such mechanisms are subject to abuse, the fact of abuse is not proof of the undesirability of the mechanism—not unless one can show that some mechanisms are inherently more abusable than others.

So we identify the democratized school organization as one in which continuous conflict is a natural and unavoidable feature of daily conduct. Each of the member elements has its own views of what constitutes an adequate school experience and each will naturally press to have its view of matters taken most into consideration. Knowing this, teachers coming into the school situation will know to expect that their views of what should be done, by whom, and when, where, and why, are likely to be different from those of their student/clients and their administrator/superiors, and all of those will differ from the parental and general community viewpoints. But that is the nature of life in a multiconstituent formal organization, and especially in one where democratic participation in decision making is getting to be more accepted.

THE CRUCIAL IMPORTANCE OF DEMOCRATIC PROCESS. The saving grace in such situations lies, if anywhere, in the full implementation of one other democratic principle, namely, that there shall be agreed-upon procedures by which conflicts are to be resolved, and that one must be careful above all to preserve those modes of conflict resolution. That means that one does not seek to destroy the opposing parties in a conflict, and one is honor bound to accept defeat in a conflict of views so long as one has had a chance to persuade others to adopt one's point of view. At the same time, one must be permitted to strive to change the minds of others so that one's views may sometime prevail. That is, one abides by majority rule, but does not therefore cease efforts to convert the present minority into a future majority. And the triumphant majority is honor bound not to interfere with or punish the minoritarians for their continuing efforts to change people's minds, so long as they conform to the majority decision while it is in effect, and so long as they use democratic means of persuasion in efforts to become a majority.

Some may read these remarks as suggesting that all matters in dispute in schools should be decided by democratic voting. But that is not the intention here. For the participation in the decisions is to be articulated, as noted earlier, in accordance with relevant levels of competence. Who is relevant for what kind of decision is, of course, itself a matter that has to be resolved through political struggle. But one can fairly hope that over time some modest consensus may be reached among the various parties. Thus, in choosing a new principal, students may be considered relevant to the extent they can help determine whether the candidate is one to whom they feel they can relate meaningfully. Teachers are relevant since they can and must judge the likelihood of adequate rapport with and guidance from their potential chief educational officer. Superintendents are relevant in assessing the formal credentials and administrative experience of the aspirant. Boards of education are relevant insofar as they must make some estimate of the extent to which the aspirant principal has managed to satisfy the three major constituent publics (students, teachers, administrators) that in most regards he or she is reasonably qualified.

But if the law finally calls for the board of education to approve a superintendent's recommendation in such matters, then there can be no democratic voting by everyone concerned. Yet, the process of consultation with students, teachers and other administrators must surely be such that each of those constituent units feels its relevant judgment has been fairly and fully taken into account. Failing that, one can hardly expect them to have much initial confidence either in the candidate or in the claims by the board of education that they have taken all relevant factors into account in making a decision.

Similarly, in deciding what is to be taught in a given classroom on a given day, one can ordinarily assume that maximum weight will be given to teachers, guided on the one hand by certain system-wide curricular requirements, and, on the other, by the identified needs, interests and readiness of their students. So, once again, while there is no structure of democratic voting about curriculum and procedures in the classroom, there is democratic participation in the mechanisms of consultation with all relevant participants.

So, too, students may be expected to want and be entitled to exercise maximum weight for their wishes and their judgments when it comes to deciding how well they are being taught; or how considerate and concerned a teacher is, how adequate are the facilities, schedules, and programs provided them; or what their extracurricular involvements should be like; or how they should dress and wear their hair; or whether there is enough flexibility in school rules to accommodate differences; or whether teachers and other supervisory personnel are sufficiently and sympathetically available to them.

In short, one can specify at least in general terms those areas of school conduct and those aspects of school issues in which the various publics who make up the school rightly enjoy varying amounts of relevance, weight and priority in decision making. One of the most frequent sources of real problems encountered in schools is the attempt by school officials to reserve for themselves exclusively the right to decide issues in which they may have little relevance, less expertise and even less understanding of what is needed. Reasonably flexible codes which allocate significant roles to students, teachers and administrators in various problem contexts help reduce the likelihood of unnecessary and destructive conflicts (as against necessary and constructive conflict). It may take a lot of pushing and shoving in a school system to get one's legitimate areas of quasi-sovereignty established. But it has been done in various places, and it can be done in others.

HOW SCHOOLS DIFFER FROM OTHER ORGANIZATIONS

We have now drawn out some of the major implications of the three major structural features of school systems, considered as large scale organizations: the fact that they are unavoidably bureaucratic, and hierarchical, and that they are made up of divergent interest groups. It remains to be noted that schools differ from almost all other formal organizations in several important regards that may prove fretful or reassuring to new teachers.

High Public Visibility and Control

First, the public school system is perhaps more publicly controlled and financed than any other major social institution, and its actions are often more highly visible and subject to public scrutiny. That means that one is literally living in a fishbowl part of the time when one is teaching.

One compensation for that is that one can always close the door to one's classroom and teach one's best without very much interference at all from anyone. A second compensation is that (for better or for worse, depending on one's values) there is community control and governance of such public institutions and that is as it should be in a democracy. When one considers how much we could all benefit from more openness in government, and in the management of other public institutions such as hospitals, libraries, museums, prisons, and police departments, one can appreciate, even if only as the lesser of two evils, the openness of schools to public view, criticism and ultimate control.

Vagueness of Criteria of Success

A second regard in which schools differ from other organizations is in the utter vagueness of what constitutes success and failure in the operation of a school. Corporations are judged by how much profit they make; prisons by how few escapes are effected; museums and libraries by how many people use their facilities; hospitals by how many sick people are processed. But no one yet can claim to have widespread agreement about what constitutes a successful education.

On one hand, that is a distressing matter. Many things would be easier if the criteria of success were the case.

On the other hand, it is a very encouraging matter, for it means, in effect, that the goals of education are always in constant and often tumultuous debate, and that is perhaps as it should be in a democratic society. For our basic notions of what we want our society to do and become are always changing, and it is altogether proper that our ideas about our schools, the most important single instrument for shaping society, should also undergo constant change. Moreover, the vagueness of the criteria of educational success and failure permits greater participation by every concerned individual, including the lay public, in attempting to shape these goals. And that too is a healthy part of democratic life.

In the face of the vague criteria of success, one can only do one's best to achieve what one thinks is important in the education venture. One also is free to advocate strongly what one believes to be important, and one must reasonably expect to win a few and lose a few during the course of such debates over the years of school experiences.

HOW TO SURVIVE IN ORGANIZATIONAL LIFE: A DOZEN RULES

With these unique features of the school as an organization now specified, we can turn to a concluding set of recommendations to the new teacher aspirants who are entering educational organization life.

They can be used in any organization in which you take up a formal status and accompanying role. But they will serve reasonably well in school systems too. They may be thought of as some maxims extracted from a primer on how to survive in an organization without really trying. For, most of them, as you will see, are things not to do, or things to avoid, rather than positive guides to powerful teaching. That is because this paper is intended as a consideration of some aspects of schools as organized systems. So, too, these injunctions I am about to issue may remind you unbearably of Polonius' speech to Laertes. That speech has traditionally been decried as insufferably Philistine. But if you are not a brave shepherd with a magic slingshot, you are best off behaving like a Philistine when in their land.

First, don't make big fights over little matters. Save your ammunition and clout, such as it may be, for things that are really worth the while. Above all, don't have an opinion on everything, even if you do. For then you will come to be known as John-who-always-argues-about-everything, or Mary-who-never-agrees-with-anything. At that point, you have lost all your possible influence.

Second, until you get tenure, let others take the formal, open lead in organizing and presenting divergent viewpoints to administrative superiors. Your viewpoints may be just, wise and important. But if you make trouble for your administrators, you are likely to be remembered, when it comes to deciding your fate, more for the trouble you make than the wisdom and sagacity and perceptiveness of your notions.

Third, you will often be judged by administrative superiors first by the extent to which you feel loyal to them, and second, and correlatively, by the extent to which you contribute to *their* success, when they are judged by their superiors. Most administrators feel wholly unappreciated by their staffs because they have the utterly unreasonable expectation that their staff members should take the "larger view" of organization needs. They seem rarely capable of understanding that they are getting paid to take that larger view but that teachers are paid for quite something else. So, the younger teachers are wise to behave in such a way as to allow their superiors to perceive them as people who do take the larger view, and do care about the organizational success, as that is judged by administrative criteria.

Fourth, most administrators prefer to have their teaching staffs "solve their own problems." Mostly that means not burdening them with problems they can't solve either, such as wildly disruptive behavior by certain students in the classroom. So if you can avoid it, don't bring or send your problem children to the office, because you will be considered incapable of adequate classroom management if you do that often.

Fifth, while everyone talks nicely about the importance of openness, creativity, imagination, discovery and the like, few administrators appreciate classroom conduct that is apparently disorderly, however creative you may think it is. You may reasonably expect that more administrators will resemble Captain Queeg than Pablo Picasso. They like neat, orderly, tight, well-run ships more often than crazy yellow submarines. So, at the outset, don't be a real swinging type whose classroom is full of gaiety, shouts, laughter, movement and creative disorder.

Sixth, don't give others grounds for negative judgments about you on trivial matters, including dress style, hair style, promptness, and other personal styles of conduct that are likely to be found offensive. While atmospheres in schools are generally much looser today than ever before, few schools have yet come to be as free and easy as college campuses. You simply can't do your own thing in schools to the same extent you did in college. For one thing, you are now considered to be serving as a model to younger children. For another, you have important and powerful colleagues and supervisors whose life styles may be significantly different and who are likely to confuse your manners with your morals. Even more important, they are likely to judge your educational desirability by your apparent moral standards. So keep your personal expressiveness to a minimum inside the schools, saving it for the privacy of your own home. Local community standards of acceptable behavior vary widely. But a good deal of what is acceptable on many college campuses will be found unacceptable by many school communities. And there are few principals or supervisory teachers whom you can expect to go to bat for you beyond a limited amount, if they come under adverse pressure from their superiors because of your publicly visible departures from community norms.

Seventh, don't assume that everyone over 25 is an irredeemable idiot or square, and that anyone in power is a knave, and that your less well-trained peers are insufferable fools. There are an incredible number of dedicated teachers in the schools throughout the country. Some of them may have styles of teaching you don't relish. But that has nothing to do with their abilities, or their concern, or their effectiveness. Some of them may dress right out of the fifties, because that's where they learned their basic styles. But, again, you know how wrong it is to judge people by their appearance, and that principle holds for people whose dress styles you can't stand as well as for your own. And if you find many of them hard to take, consider every once in a while how hard it must be for them to take you. So, be generous in your acceptance of different styles of speech, conduct, dress and interpersonal relations, which means simply let others be as different, without being sneered at, as you would want them to let you be. You above all have a strong vested interest in supporting the notion of the acceptability of a wide range of variation in personal styles, including teaching styles. For, being the newest and youngest entries into the field, you are likely to be the most variant of all.

Eighth, don't expect most of your colleagues to be as freshly attuned to the newest findings in your subject matter field as you are and don't flaunt your fresh learning at them. For, in defense, they will counter with their "wisdom" gained through "long experience" about how best to teach things. They may often invoke that experience anyway. And they may often be right. For many people do learn lots of things of value from long years of experience, even if many others learn little of value except how to be rigid about their preconceptions. But don't assume you have nothing to learn from experienced teachers. They may have a great deal to teach you, if you are open to learn from them. So, don't hesitate to go to older teachers for help with problems. You will probably need such help often. Others will be pleased and flattered you came to them, and you will probably find you can get some real help.

The same considerations apply to your relationships to administrators. Don't assume they are simply political hacks who have gotten where they are for no good reasons. There are lots of foolish things done in choosing people for educational leadership, but the screening and selection process probably operates as well and as soundly in schools as in any other organization. And while administrators do want you to be loyal and be a good team member, according to their own rights, many of them also want to do a good job of education. They take pride in quality education. Assume that pride to be present and go to them for help, without being a burden. You will learn over time how to need and secure the assistance of others without their feeling burdened by you or without their thinking you incompetent. It's much better, both for your own learning and for your organizational survival, to be seen, and correctly so, as someone who is eager to learn and who asks for help, rather than to be seen as a know-it-all.

Ninth, you will find plenty of teachers and administrators who simply don't pull their own weight in the school. They goof off. They teach the same foolish things in the same foolish ways year in and out. These are the tired ones; the ones who are worn out; the disillusioned ones; the apathetic ones. They are to be found in every school, in every profession, in every organization. (Tenure makes it possible for schools to have a higher percentage of such people than do most other organizations, where people can be fired quietly for incompetence. But tenure also protects *competent* teachers from being fired for arbitrary reasons of administrative displeasure.) So don't imitate the worst members of the staff because you will quickly get to hate teaching.

Remember, too, that in any organization of humans, the least moral member of the organization will drag the general level of conduct down to the lowest common denominator, unless he is otherwise restrained. The same principle applies to levels of competence and conscientiousness. So, you can be as gung-ho as you want to be, even though some of the older, disillusioned time servers will sneer at you.

Tenth, work as hard as you can to make effective contact with students, but never choose a course of action simply because it may please them any more than you would choose one simply because it will displease them. You can properly care a great deal about being liked by your students. But if you have to choose between being liked as against being admired, respected, and valued for how and what you teach, by all means choose the admiration, respect, and value of things. One of the very best evaluations you can get from students is the judgment that you are tough and fair and a good teacher, even though that excludes the possibility that they will look on you as a friend and as someone they can invite to their parties and have a good time with. You can properly be friendly and warm with students. But you can't properly be friends with them, not in the same sense that people of the same age can be friends. Don't try to swing with the kids. You will look damn foolish!

Eleventh, don't take on roles you have no experience with. That means don't play at counselor, psychoanalyst, love adviser. If students feel free to come to you for personal help, don't get to know too much about their personal lives. Do refer them to others who are more skilled. That means, too, don't encourage rebellion against parents, police, or other authority figures. You never know what the psychic balance of a young person is at any given time, and giving wise advice to young, troubled people requires extraordinary seriousness, good training and deep wisdom. The best help you can give to young students is to refer them to the proper person or agency, and to encourage them sympathetically to go get help if they seem to need it. You may be flattered into thinking you really know what the kids need. But that would be a very serious mistake on your part in 99 out of 100 cases.

Twelfth, if you find many practices you would like to change, you will be effective in proportion to the extent you keep these things in mind.

- Be sure to distinguish between your private passions, that is, what would please you personally, and good public policy, that is, the general good for most other people, especially students. No democratic society can survive very long or very well if everyone tries to have public policy reflect the fullness of his or her private preferences, tastes and passions.
- Don't go overboard for educational fads in the name of being innovative. Anyone can be innovative. It is as easy as doing the same old thing. Change is no more virtuous than stability. New things are not inherently better than old things, or vice versa. The schools have been plagued as much with so-called innovations, announced and touted in apocalyptic terms, as with traditional rigidities. Almost all of the innovations have proven to be duds.

55

No single change in a school's organization is likely to be able to make very much of a difference. But little differences may nevertheless be very important to try to make. So, don't start out by claiming too much for your proposed change and you won't be too disillusioned when the actual size of difference proves to be rather modest—if you are very lucky. So, too, every change is sure to have some negative consequences for some people and some values, in addition to whatever positive consequences it has for others. Sensible innovation takes account of both positive and negative consequences, insofar as they can be foreseen, and chooses on the basis of wisely weighed balances of net gain.

- Everytime you try to change something in the schools, you are sure to be challenging and disturbing some well-established habits, including attitudes, practices and schedules. Such habits are rather difficult to change. If you don't believe that, take some of your most favored habits and ask how easy it would be for you to change them. Then you will understand more fully why you will surely encounter resistance whenever you try to shake up other people's habits.

- Older people don't like to be told how to live and behave by younger people any more than younger people like to be told those things by older people. If you are going to be effective in introducing changes, you had better get yourself some allies from the other side of the age lines, so that you don't polarize the older vs. the younger members of the staff.

- A lot of people have a lot of ego invested in the ways they have become accustomed to doing things. If you can't understand that, a little introspection will once again reveal to you how much ego you have invested in your ideas about how things ought to be done. So, count on at least as much irrational, ego-laden resistance to proposals for change as you would probably yourself offer if someone came vigorously charging after your own favorite habits. And you had better figure out some ways in which you can save the faces and egos of potential opponents so that they can consider your proposals without fear of degradation and humiliation.

Thirteenth, as Polonius said, "This above all, to thine own self be true." But, if you believe that to be a proper imperative for your own conduct, you would be wise to assume that *most other people believe they are operating in accordance with the same perspective.*

FINALE: WHY IT MAY ALL BE WORTH THE WHILE

You may resent all these little pieces of guidance. But you may find them a little more acceptable if you remember that most public school systems have the preposterous rule that tenure is to be decided at the beginning of the third or fourth year of teaching. I believe it a preposterous rule because no sound judgment can be made in such a short time. But the rule is there. And once you survive the tenure judgment, you can move more resolutely and boldly to make a real difference in the life of the school and in the general educational policies of your community. So, being on your best behavior for a few years may seem worth the while, when you consider what is at stake, and when you further take into account that the classroom teacher is the single most important social multiplier agent in the whole society. Who else can seriously affect the minds and hearts of literally tens of thousands of people during a lifetime career? Your salary may be abominably low; your community prestige not much higher; and interference by others in your conduct may be sometimes at an intolerable level. But in the long run, it is what you do in the classroom that matters. And if you do it well, it can matter a great deal to thousands of young people.

Section 3: Hierarchy and Egalitarianism: The Case for the Study of Organizations in the Education of Teachers: An Organizer's View

Girard D. Hottleman

THE NEED

That teachers do not study organizations is in itself a lesson in the worth and function of organizations. Organizations exist for two purposes: to oppose an adversary greater than an individual or to permit the individual to achieve objectives that require the use of resources exceeding the limits of an individual. If there were no adversaries or no objectives that required greater-than-personal resources to achieve, there would be no organizations.

It can be assumed that curricula for students in preparation for entry into the teaching profession are designed to meet needs based on an analysis of what teachers do in their practice. Because the study of organizations is not usually included in teacher preparation programs, it must be assumed that those who analyze teacher needs do not consider that teachers, in the ordinary practice of the profession, oppose adversaries greater than themselves or set objectives the achievement of which requires the use of resources exceeding the limits of an individual. The same observation can be made about inservice education, which is generally controlled by school administrations. In fact, this may be even more worth noting in light of observations that will be made later in this discussion.

It is well known, however, both through experience and analysis, that teachers teach as components of a learning system that is in itself an organization. It is also well known that the resources for the survival and proper functioning of the learning systems (organizations) that we call schools derive from interaction with communities, which also are organizations. Further, learning objectives for children are organized system wide and are obtainable only through relationships between individual teachers and other components of the system. This is additional evidence of the organizational nature of schools. The evidence that teaching is a by-product of organization is so clear and so overwhelming that it becomes impossible to attribute the neglect of organizational study to an oversight on the part of those who plan the education of teachers. The neglect of organizational study in teacher preparation programs, then, must be seen as purposeful rather than accidental.

If knowledge of organizational functioning is an essential skill for successful teaching, why would it be almost universally omitted from teacher preparation programs? Perhaps the best way to answer this question is to consider the consequences if such were not the case, to consider what would occur if teachers were as well trained in organizational expertise as in their subject specialties or learning methods.

In organizational terms teachers currently are loosely connected elements of a system/organization (school or school district) that is in turn a component of a larger organization (the community). The hierarchy of control is downward from the community, to the elected community representatives, to administrators, to the school, to the teacher. Teachers, in this perspective, are the end product of the political process rather than the shapers of the political process.

In order to fully understand the implications of this, it is necessary to look not only at the teachers' function as components of the system, but more importantly at their role independent of system relationship. It is unfortunate from the perspective of the teachers' consciousness that in the drive toward professionalization of teachers, the debate over whether teachers are professional or not has centered on achieved personal attributes—autonomy, education required, certification, etc.—rather than the role. If the lengthy debate had instead occurred on role, it would now be very well known that teachers are probably the prime profession rather a secondary one. If one were to argue the value of a profession by the breadth and depth of its social impact, physicians and attorneys, now considered of superior significance relative to teachers in the social hierarchy, would come off second best. Physicians come in contact with members of society only periodically and for limited reasons, usually a malfunction of the organism. Similarly, attorneys have relatively infrequent contact with members of society. They enter into a client relationship only when there is a social malfunction.

Further, physicians practice their art within the framework of existing societal conditions—it is no more difficult to heal a fascist than it is to heal an egalitarian. The practice of law is also the exercise of the status quo. In their professional lives, even the most strident libertarian attorneys do not often argue the merits of a law, but rather give their attention to the interpretation and application of law.

On the other hand, consider the teacher. Teachers don't deal with isolated members of society on rare occasions. All of society flows into contact with the teaching profession for enormous periods of time and around the most crucial events. The crystallization of values; the shaping of attitudes; the development of perception, creativity, and intelligence; all are functions of the educational process. Medicine determines who shall live and who shall die; law determines who shall pay and who shall be paid; but education determines the very nature of society and in so doing creates the framework within which all occupations and professions can function. In light of all this, it is not mysterious that universities and schools become the first targets of oppression or the vanguard of revolution during periods of social instability. It is also not difficult to understand the enormous energies that Nazi Germany deployed into the Hitler Youth Movement, the missionary and parochial school movements characteristic of large religions, or as a matter of fact, the pervasive government interest in American public education. In all of these instances and in others that could be cited, there is a recognition by those in established power that the values that created their power must be continued if their power is to be maintained. Those who find it difficult to believe this assumption need only look at the nature of the education that established governments (organizations) support. The Hitler Youth Movement did not include deep indoctrination in the principles of constitutional democracy; the Catholic missionary and parochial school movements did not include heavy doses of comparative religion; those who fund the American public schools do not encourage programs on Communism, revolutionary tactics, or atheism; and if we can focus for a moment on other educational movements within our culture, large established American youth movements such as the Scouts, DeMolay and Rainbow, various Cadet programs, etc., foster order, hierarchy, obedience, and the like, not individual rights, personal ethics, and creative consciences. When the day arrives that public schools offer courses in lesbian liberation, alternatives to the Christian ethic, open marriage, civil disobedience, etc., tax support will dry up; and when the Boy Scouts of America organize their members not in antilitter campaigns, but into political cells that sponsor sit-ins and demonstrations in federal buildings against whatever war we are engaged in at any given time, it is a certainty that they will lose their "respect," their nonprofit tax status, and their free advertising on television.

These somewhat diverting comments are made only in the interest of demonstrating the significance of mass youth education movements such as the American public schools, and hence the significance of the American school teacher. In the teachers' hands are entrusted not the physical health of the culture, nor the policing of the system of justice of the culture, but the entire shape and future of the culture. The culture will be, in large measure, what teachers determine. This is the greatest responsibility that a culture can delegate, and this is why I assert that teaching is probably a more significant profession than is usually recognized.

This is also why, to return to our original thesis, the study of organization is excluded from would be teachers' established training programs. Those who know too much about organization cannot be trusted to hold the society still. Let us look at organization to see why.

THE THEORY

Knowledge of organizations is important to the extent that one wishes to invest one's life either in the concentration or the distribution of power. I define power as the ability to reach self-selected goals. With power, more goals or broader goals can be achieved. As power is reduced, goals become reduced or limited. Freedom, then, becomes a function of power, and restriction a function of lack of power. These principles hold true whether one's self-selected goals are for oneself alone or for others. The capacity to do good is also a function of power. With power, one can do good; without power, one can only wish good.

Strangely enough, even in a democratic society such as ours, in social institutions/organizations power is narrow at the base and wide at the top. Most of our social institutions are structured into a vertical hierarchy in layers, like a pyramid of people. The more populated the layer, the less power it has, the converse also holds. For example, there are more teachers than principals, yet principals have more power than teachers; there are more principals than superintendents of schools, yet superintendents have more power than principals. This principle—power in social institutions resides in inverse proportion to population layers— is widespread. Only my cautious instincts, resident from my formal logic days, prevent me from declaring it universal. It even carries into the political arena where, in theory, checks and balances exist to equalize power. The fact is, however, that the veto power of presidents and governors compels the mobilization of enormous energy by lower-level power figures to overcome the power of the uppermost figure. The theory is to balance power. The practice is that it is not balanced; the will of one person overcomes the will of many.

Without too much fear of refutation, then, it can be asserted that social institutions/organizations in America are not egalitarian models. Egalitarianism is a social system in which power and resources are equally distributed and the ability to realize goals is identical for all members of the system. This certainly is not the American way. Those who wish to realize goals within American institutions have three alternatives: climb to the top, gain favor with the top, or compel the top to cooperate.

The top of the people pyramid is precarious, but pleasant. To have power is to be able to make the rules, dispense the resources, promulgate sanctions, act without explanation, and satisfy oneself more rapidly and more fully than anyone else in the system. In America it means more money, more status, more freedom, more accoutrements, etc. It also means more competition, more antagonism, more visibility, and more interest on the part of others; all combined, more paranoia. It would be fair to assert that as one rises in power within a social system, both one's freedom and one's vulnerability increase. Increased freedom is a direct function of increased power. Increased vulnerability is not a direct function of increased power, but of increased desire. Those at the top have much to lose, and there are many who would help them lose it. As a consequence, the more there is at stake, the more vulnerability exists because with power comes the knowledge that there are detractors and attackers and if they succeed, the pain of reduced freedom and satisfaction must be endured.

A look at the bottom of the pyramid gives a different view. Those with less power have fewer benefits, there is nothing to lose. In warfare, even in social warfare, which is an apt description of life within organizations, this is an advantage—defeat means nothing more than to maintain the paucity of established benefits. This is quite another perspective than the view from the top. Those without power value those who can get them power; those with power value those who can help them maintain power. What is appealing to one level of power, then, is repugnant to another. The value contrasts that exist within organizations give some clues to ways in which organizations can be made to function in more egalitarian ways. The ordinary pattern of behavior in organizations is that those at the top desire stabilization of things as they are; those at the bottom desire change. Change that promises to distribute power threatens those at the top; it gives hope to those at the bottom.

Because of the survival needs of power figures, proposed changes that threaten to diminish their power are rejected. Changes that increase their power are admitted into the system. In light of this, the tools of abstract reason, logic, evidence, etc., are often impotent, and it is because of this that organizations often become insensitive and irrational. Further, to argue for changes in system behavior based on client improvement is also often fruitless. On the other hand, to advocate changes based on the improvement of the status of power figures is often productive. The real question becomes, then, what to do when changes needed in the system to benefit clients or lower-level power figures come into conflict with the survival needs of power figures.

We now come, I think, to the reason for the neglect of organizational study in the normal education of a teacher (or a social service worker or a nurse, etc.). To understand organization is to understand conflict. And to understand conflict is to understand how to diminish the power of power figures. In a word, if theory and application of conflict were widely taught and understood, society and its institutions would move much more steadily toward the egalitarian means than they now do. On the other hand, if in place of hard conflict theory, we substitute the values inherent in respect for authority, channels of command, titles, rank, respect for institutions, hierarchy, emblems, badges, medals, and stripes social stratification, "acceptable" manners, dress, gestures, and languages, etc., egalitarianism becomes more of a distant abstraction than a present reality. An examination of most of our education reveals that the result, if not the object of education, is social stratification—the preservation of the established order rather than the wholesale encouragement of changing established conditions.

The question of this paper—Why study organization?—really gets down to: Why study conflict? The answer is that only through conflict can power concentrations be broken up and distributed more evenly. Only through conflict can teachers gain power for themselves or their clients. Hence, the realization of the goals of teachers and students lies in the study of organizations, the study of conflict. Let us turn now to an examination of conflict in order to understand why knowledge of conflict is so dangerous to established authority and power in our society that it has been almost universally purged from the consciousness of the culture.

THE PRACTICE

Relationships between individuals and groups within organizations can be characterized as harmonious, competitive, or conflictual. Harmony exists when there is agreement on both ends and means. Competition exists when there is agreement on ends, but not means. Conflict exists when there is disagreement about ends. When conflict arises, unless power balancing forces emerge, it will ordinarily be resolved by fiat of the most powerful figure in the conflict, especially if the approved resolution is of significant to the survival of the most powerful figure. This means that in conflict relationships it is important either to be the most powerful figure or to reduce the power of the most powerful figure in order to resolve the conflict in one's favor. Our training suggests that conflict can be resolved through dialogue, consensus, accommodation, or compromise. These processes are sometimes effective in harmonious or competitive relationships or when functioning with peers. They are not, however, generally effective in conflict relationships between figures of varying power.

Within our society, nonconflict relationships are generally held to be superior to conflict relationships. Before we examine the tactical principles of conflict, it is important to understand some of the roots of the intense and pervasive negative social attitude that exists about the nature of conflict. Keep in mind that because power and authority generate downward within our social institutions, conflict must be viewed as a challenge to accepted social order. Those who are dissatisfied with established order—the disaffected, the disenfranchised, the victims of the system, etc.—are those who benefit least by it. Those who are content are those who benefit most. When conflict erupts, then, if it is not resolved in favor of those whom the system benefits, a shift in power or benefits results. The result of such a shift is always detrimental to those at the uppermost levels of the institutional pyramid and always beneficial to those at the lower levels. Those with power stand to lose in conflict; those without power stand to gain.

We have seen that in the context of organizations at least, freedom, access to benefits, and self-realization are functions of power and that the opposite conditions are functions of powerlessness. Power, therefore, is a good. We have also seen that power is obtained through conflict. If conflict is the route to power and power is good, why, then, is conflict so universally held as destructive and repugnant, even by those whom it benefits?

The answer to this puzzling question is complex and deserves a separate study all to itself. Without diffusing the focus of this discussion, let me suggest a few of the possible major origins of this prevailing paradoxical attitude. A generous (if not somewhat depressing) interpretation would be that our society so values social order (or needs it for survival) that it inculcates a deep anticonflict attitude in order to preserve or at least stabilize institutions, even if this means significant and permanent deprivation of members of society. Another possible interpretation is that although the results of conflict benefit some members of society, other members are harmed in the process, and the Christian-Judaic ethic so prohibits the harming of others that it is thought to be superior virtue to endure suffering rather than to induce suffering. Without presenting supporting evidence, however, I will advance the hypothesis that the prevailing attitude that conflict is a destructive mode of human relationships is a natural and logical result of hierarchical societies and the hierarchical institutions that mirror the society at large. We cannot discard the impact of the long history of humans and their governments and institutions. From the knowledge we have, stretching from our beginnings to the present, we know of no instance of an egalitarian society. All societies have had stratified power. Forms and philosophies have varied, but the essential structure has always been that there are a few who have much and many who have little. Primitive tribes heaped rewards and honor on their chiefs and shamans. Monarchies, republics, democracies, dictatorships, socialist and communist societies in every place at every time, from the Greek Republic with its slave labor, to the Roman Empire, to the Egyptian and Babylonian Empires, to European aristocracies, to the South American republics, Russian communism, and the American democracy—all have been characterized by the layers of the elite superimposed on and supported by large layers of the deprived. Our history is so universal on this point that we could be led to consider that it is the natural human condition. I assert that it is not. What has happened, if we can return from a quick glance at history to the American public schools, is that those in power are the shapers of society and much of the shaping is done by the institutions over which they have power. The shaping is done by making certain that the products of institutions, in the example of schools, children, manifest support for prevailing (establishment) needs and attitudes. Those who achieve authority in social institutions (schools) are selected on the basis of their commitment to directing the institution toward that end, and are rewarded with higher salaries, prestige, and power for their efforts. Success, then, becomes a function of mirroring the values and attitudes of those with power. In this way those who are established in power become not only the shapers of society and its institutions, but also the gatekeepers of social mobility. From those out of power, those with power select for advancement or elevation only the people who have learned the values of the powerful and accepted the mission of preserving the status quo.

The system into which teachers enter, then, is quite different than what they have been led to believe. They themselves, and the teachers and professors who have produced them, have been trained in a system in which conflict is seen as destructive, individualistic behavior as suspect, and conformity to reigning hierarchical values as a virtue. They have been rewarded for conformity, punished for nonconformity. They have seen success for students, for teachers, for workers, for their parents, for practically everyone, occur as a result of sublimating personal impulses to the benefit of the objectives of controlling authorities. But somehow, even with massive experience to the contrary, some teachers enter teaching with the belief that the purpose of the schools is to answer the intellectual, physical, and emotional needs of children. It is at the point of discovering that this is not true that school conflict begins, and it is also at this point that teachers discover how inadequately their conditioning and their education (more accurately, their lack of education) have prepared them for the battle. The initial awakening is often produced when the teacher becomes aware of the contradiction between the expressed rhetoric about schools and the schools' behavior.

Teachers new to teaching find inadequate preventive, diagnostic, or remedial programs and facilities available to meet the needs of their children. They find inflexible policies that inhibit individualization, and they find that exceptions to rules exist for the privileged. They find prejudicial tracking, punitive grading and discipline systems, and demands made on children that do not relate to their physical, matura-tional, or motivational readiness. They find that the value system of the schools derives from institutional needs rather than the needs of children. The learning experience is often made secondary to adminis-trative needs. When they attempt to correct such contradictions through requests, through dialogue, through reason, through evidence, through channels, they are repulsed and defeated. When they attack frontally, they are censured and condemned. When they organize for an attack, they are generally trounced in the attempt. Eventually, after a sufficient number of experiences ending in frustration and failure, those who began their careers as sensitive advocates for the rights and needs of children fall back exhausted and routinely perform the sanctioned tasks of the system. This state of passive acceptance is the inevitable result of the destructive erosion of repeated failure. Better knowledge of conflict dynamics would reduce the frequency of failure and the number of idealist casualties, and it would enable teachers who come into conflict over worthy objectives to prevail more frequently than they now do. Let us examine, then, the rules for success through conflict.

Consider first the power structure of a typical hierarchically structured organization/institution/school system.

Figure 1: *Hierarchically structured organization.*
Legend: *SB = School Board; S = Superintendent;*
P = Principals; T = Teachers.

As cited earlier, the flow of power in institutions such as that illustrated in Figure 1 is from the top down even though population decreases from bottom to top. Decision makers at any level of the pyramid have power over those affected below, but not those above, so that the impact of decisions ripples downward in institutions, not upward. Because of this, one of the first principles of organizational conflict is to attack problems at a power level above the cause of the conflict. For example, if a principal institutes a repressive policy, demands from below do not have the capacity to modify his or her behavior. The principal's interest lies in gaining approval from those who have power over him or her, not in gaining approval from those under whom he or she has power. If on the other hand, someone above directs the principal to modify his or her behavior, he or she must do so. The key to the principal's behavior, then, is the superintendent, and the key to the superintendent's behavior is the school board, etc.

The question then comes, how to motivate a power figure to direct a subordinate to act. If the analysis so far is correct—that power figures act, especially on significant issues, according to their personal survival needs and that the benefit of their actions to lower-level power figures is accidental to their behavior—then arguments to upper-level power figures based on the needs of the lower elements of the system are not effective. If what is needed is a reduction in a power figure's strength or resources, then that power figure must be made to understand that the decision to erode his or her power is the only means by which he or she can survive at all. This concept expresses itself in the principle that power shifts in conflict relationships occur when the pain (damage, loss, etc.) of holding power is greater than the pain of letting it go. Clearly, then, what is needed in a battle with a power figure is the capacity to bring harm or do damage. Harm is always subjectively perceived; what is harmful to one power figure may not be harmful to another. However, the abstract principle is that behavior by an antagonist is seen as harmful when it is perceived as a possible threat to survival. One component that is universal in the formula is that to fall out of favor with one's superiors is threatening to survival. The remainder of the formula is derived from an analysis of the antagonist's ambitions and fears. Once these are detected, they become the basis for creating the direction of the tactical assault. If a power figure values money, then one threatens his or her purse; if a power figure is ambitious, one threatens to reduce his or her capacity to achieve those ambitions, etc. In all events, however, all power figures are sustained by higher figures; they do not stand alone. To cut off that sustenance is the primary tactical objective in social warfare.

How do those with less power establish a position strong enough to provide a real threat to those with more power? Knowledge of organizations and organizing provides the answer. In the context of this discussion I define an organizer as one who first congeals powerless figures with diffused strength into a mass in which the diffused strength becomes concentrated and who then directs the newly congealed mass toward the vulnerable points of the power figure adversary in such a way as to achieve the desired objective.

The use of semantics borrowed from the science of physical properties is not accidental. There is a physics that operates in social institutions that is as sure as the physics of mechanics.

THE PHYSICS OF ORGANIZING

No matter how powerful or wealthy any one person or any group of persons becomes in any form of society, neither power nor wealth can ever be greater than the sum of the power and wealth of the whole society. The organizer (read: social reformer) must learn to view any society or subset of society (institution/organization) as an imbalanced seesaw with power and wealth on one end and deprivation on the other. The key question in organizational work is: What force must be exerted on the disadvantaged side of the seesaw in order to cause the necessary downward shift in power and money to the deprived? The primary method is unity of the organized. Success consists in mobilizing the disadvantaged to the degree necessary to counter their disadvantage. To state the principle at its extreme: If the entire American population of 210 million were marshalled against the President of the United States, the President would fall. The pressure of 210 million people with all of their resources marshalled against a single official would be sufficient to upset the most powerful figure in history. But in a system such as the United States, must all 210 million be organized? No? Well, if not all 210 million, how many and with what force and over what period of time and to what end? Would 200 million do? Or 100 million or 60 million or 10,000 of the right people or the right forces? These are the questions the organizer must deal with.

Consider the condition at the beginning of a campaign as stasis. Regardless of the level or extent of power at either end of the social spectrum, no matter how many are advantaged or disadvantaged or to what degree, prior to the entrance of the organizer, all societies must for the organizer's purpose be considered imbalanced. This applies to Devil's Island as well as the most peaceful Trappist Monastery. It applies to a traditional ladies' club as much as it does to a fascist army completely geared up for war. And from the perspective of this discussion, it applies to the public schools.

The campaign begins with an assessment of the objective. Generically, all objectives require a shift of power from one side of the seesaw to the other. All objectives can be defined as realistic, provided that they do not demand more in their attainment than is present in the total system. Their achievement, however, is a direct function of two factors—how much power is at stake in the desired shift and how much energy must be exerted to shift the desired power the desired distance. A complete shift or reversal in power requires maximum energy; a partial or minor shift requires less energy; stasis requires no energy. All social systems have built-in resistors to sustain impulse variables; the greater the desirability or necessity of the element of power, the greater the sustaining ability of the resistors. In the organizer's terms, this means that the energy he or she must produce to achieve an objective will be a direct function of the resistance capacity attached to the element under attack. Usually, resistance capacity attached to a systems element varies directly with the perceived importance of the systems element to the survival of the system. The more important something is to the establishment, the more difficult it is to take away; the less important it is, the easier it is to take away. For example, in a factory campaign, the workers have three objectives: (a) to change the colors of their aprons from blue to orange; (b) to increase their wages; and (c) to require that the factory owner step down and permit joint and equal ownership by all the workers in the factory. Given the ordinary course of events, the energy necessary to achieve the first objective is less than needed for the remaining two. The energy required to achieve the third objective would be enormous because it offers the maximum threat to the survival of the locus of power and would be met with the greatest resistance.

The effective organizer recognizes distinctions between objectives, assesses the resistance capacity, and galvanizes energy above the resistance point in order to achieve the objective. It is important to remember that how important an element is to the survival of an establishment force is a matter of the perception of the establishment, not the perception of the disestablished.

A paradox exists in the principles of analysis of human systems that is not necessarily paralleled in physical systems; whatever is most desired or needed by those in power, although the need for its continuance will cause them to mobilize the greatest resistance, it nevertheless becomes their most vulnerable point. In simpler terms, whatever people want makes them vulnerable, and whatever they want most makes them most vulnerable. This statement is true because greater compromise results from the threat of total destruction than from the threat of partial destruction. The truth of the statement can probably best be understood by stating its negative: Whatever people want least makes them least vulnerable—because all exchanges in a power system come through bargaining and if nothing is valued, no exchange can be offered. Safety ultimately rests in having nothing or wanting nothing. Vulnerability exists in having something or wanting something, and the degree of possession or desire determines the degree of vulnerability. For this reason David Rockefeller is more vulnerable than the welfare recipient; likewise, the ascetic is more secure and untouchable than the committed and successful hedonist.

Reality might seem to contradict this principle because the Rockefellers have survived admirably for four generations, but their survival is less evidence of their invulnerability than it is evidence of the ineffectiveness of organizers to exploit their vulnerability. The enormously advantaged position of the Rockefellers has accrued from the relatively uninhibited manipulation and exploitation of huge holdings of wealth through such instruments as the Chase Manhattan Bank and Standard Oil. But neither Chase Manhattan nor Standard Oil can survive without the willing compliance of thousands of employees who produce the surpluses of wealth through these instruments and place them at the disposal of the Rockefellers. To state the point simply: If all (or most) of the employees of Chase Manhattan refused to work or refused to work under conditions that created a surplus, the advantaged position of the Rockefellers would be diminished. This event has not occurred either because no organizer has desired it or because none was capable of pulling it off. Because it has not happened, however, is not proof that it cannot happen. In terms of this essay, continued success of the Rockefeller family in sustaining a position of relative advantage is proof only that they are superior organizers to those who would see it otherwise.

It might be well at this point while we are examining the principles of organizational physics to follow the progress of an imbalanced system as it moves from stasis to turmoil and from there attains either a new stasis or returns to the old stasis under the response of the system to turmoil. The following diagrams are offered as helpful analogies.

Consider a large system in stasis (Diagram 1), imbalanced by the compacted weight of those who have accumulated power and wealth on one side (A) and the dispersed and diffuse weight of those who are unrelated, powerless, and poor on the other side (B). In the case of schools, A represents the school board or the superintendent, and B represents the teachers or the students or interested community figures.

Diagram 1.

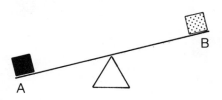

Confronted with such an imbalanced system, the organizer has two alternatives (or combinations of both). On the one hand, the organizer can diffuse the compacted power (Diagram 2), thus effecting balance. This is done by breaking up relationships between power figures or by separating them from resources, authority, or money.

Diagram 2.

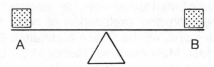

Or the organizer can bring about a compactness to the diffuse side (Diagram 3). This is done by solidifying the disaffected behind an issue.

Diagram 3.

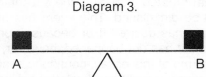

A mixed effect (Diagram 4) will cause the same result.

Diagram 4.

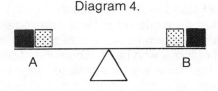

Any attempt by the organizer to bring balance into an imbalanced social system will be countered by attempts of the compacted power elements to maintain stasis. One method (Diagram 5) is to attempt to counter consolidation moves by adding on additional resources.

Diagram 5.

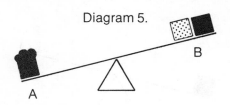

Reserves are brought in; new coalitions are formed; resources from other imbalanced systems are borrowed. The establishment reaches out into the community to join forces with sympathetic groups. Thus, for example, in a labor model, if we were to attempt to cripple the beef industry by closing down the feed market, industry response might be to import feed. If labor counters by closing down the ports, industry might counter by flying in the feed.

If all counters can be countered or if the establishment efforts to counter becomes unprofitable, then a second move can be brought into play. Established power, when threatened, can attract key elements of the opposition to its side, thus maintaining imbalance (Diagram 6). This is done commonly by recruiting persons of talent or intelligence or leadership out of the opposition.

Diagram 6.

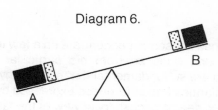

Another technique is to split any attempts at compactness (Diagram 7), thus recreating the original diffusion and preventing countervailing thrusts. This is done through a variety of divide-and-conquer strategies and through the use of threat, selective advantage, propaganda, etc.

Diagram 7.

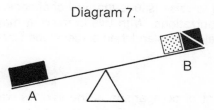

The principles, then, are relatively simple; it is the complexity and variety of the techniques for applying the principles that make the achievement of organizational change so difficult. The essential principle, above all else, is that those who wish to do good through the power of organizations must learn to solidify the disaffected elements within the institution into a countervailing force in order to achieve parity of power. Further, they must learn to sustain the force of solidarity and to direct it in a tactical way. Without such knowledge the force of good can only be rhetoric, and in hierarchical institutions rhetoric is music to the ears of the establishment. Clearly, there is a case for the intense study of organizational behavior in the education of teachers, and perhaps paradoxically, such a program of study will never become a reality until teachers organize to make sure it happens.

Section 4: Commentary:
Some Reflections on Issues Raised
in the Three Discussions

Roy A. Edelfelt   Ronald G. Corwin

Each author has chosen to concentrate on a few features of schools as organizations and does so from his particular perspective. The themes developed are so fundamental that it is worthwhile to reflect further upon the similarities and differences expressed by the authors. Further discussion also seems necessary in view of the fact that this is still a controversial field. Even theorists who agree on the basics will differ on specific points. People looking for quick and simple answers may find this state of the art unsatisfying. But on the positive side, it means that each of us, as students of organization, may have something worthwhile to say. Indeed, the purpose of this volume is to present alternative perspectives, and to raise issues that will challenge each of us to think further about organizations. With this in mind, it may now be useful to compare some major ideas and themes developed by the three writers.

APPROACHES

The first point of comparison is the various ways the authors approach the subject. Lortie and Tumin are sociologists and students of organizations. They describe educational organizations. In addition, Tumin offers some advice designed to help individuals achieve success in organizations. As we interpret his comments, he is not defending the requirements for survival. He is realistic about how most people do, and often must, act to prosper or be promoted in the average organization.

By taking a descriptive approach, these authors have been able to identify several key features of schools, such as their cellular bureaucratic structure, compulsory attendance, local financing, hierarchical structure, stress on maintaining discipline, their multiple constituencies and the reasons for their large size.

Hottleman takes another tack. His discussion will appeal especially to people who are tired of conforming and impatient for change. As an advocate of change, he wants organizational reform through the strategy of collective teacher action. This prescriptive approach has some disadvantages in that it presents only a particular focus and gives a partial view of schools. Power and conflict are very important, but they are not the only characteristics of schools. However, the approach has fundamental advantages as well. It illuminates the process of conflict in a way that is not possible in a purely descriptive treatment. It can help us understand schools better and suggest ways to improve them. Thus, Hottleman's discussion is stimulating and thought provoking.

IMAGE OF ORGANIZATIONS

The three authors take different perspectives which lead them to adopt slightly different images of organization. Tumin starts with the larger picture, the macrocosm, and calls attention to the large scale, bureaucratic nature of school districts, stressing their structural features and the forces favoring large scale systems. Lortie starts from another vantage point. His view of schools is comprehensive, but his focus is on classrooms, which he sees as the basic part from which the larger system of schools and school districts emerge. Thinking of schools as collections of classrooms, he observes that authority follows vertical lines only within *managerial* spheres. This leaves teachers in charge of the educational process within classrooms.

Hottleman is concerned about change and how it can be achieved through collective action. He chooses to concentrate on the locus of power and the managerial hierarchy. His position is that this hierarchy, as presently arranged, is detrimental to teachers unless they organize to protect themselves. He is concerned about power but gives less attention than Lortie to the teachers' authority over the classroom.

THE USEFULNESS OF ORGANIZATIONS

To Tumin, organizations are the end products of the impersonal forces of evolution. He contends that bureaucratic structure and hierarchy have proven to be necessary and useful, their utility often outweighing the problems they create. By contrast, Hottleman zeros in on their negative qualities. He seems to have in mind the "monstrous model of organization" to which Tumin refers. Hierarchy is seen as opressive and conspiratorial. Thus, he accuses teacher educators of deliberately depriving teachers of organizational theory to keep teachers in their place. Lortie appreciates the utility of organizations, but also makes observations that might be construed as a measured and reasonable argument for change. The difference in perception between the scholar and the user of knowledge in these papers in instructive. We leave the important synthesizing task to you as you attempt to apply theoretical concepts in action settings.

SOURCES OF PROBLEMS

Because bureaucracy is a relatively efficient form of organization, Tumin concludes that whenever bureaucracies fail to function well, it is probably due to the failure of their members to perform as prescribed and expected. He sees many sources of malfunction: unrealistic expectations, inadequate resources, poorly developed incentives, inadequate training and socialization, inflexible supervision, and confusion of roles and lines of communication.

All three authors appreciate the structural problems that can arise in bureaucracies. Hottleman wants to change the balance of power and authority as a way of alleviating some of the problems of teachers. Lortie takes an even more global position when he suggests that many of the problems in schools can be traced to their cellular structure and poorly developed technology, as well as to the hierarchy. What seems ironic is that the leaders of teacher organizations who are responsible for bargaining contracts do not seem inclined to bargain collectively for structural reform of schools. Even Hottleman makes no mention of such an approach despite his strong position on action for change.

THE DEGREE OF AUTONOMY AND STRUCTURAL LOOSENESS

Theoretically, complex organizations are made up of distinct parts, or groupings of people and tasks that constitute the division of labor. "Slippage" tends to take place as policies are implemented at successive levels of authority and in different zones of the organization. Lortie stresses this feature when he refers to schools as "cellular" structures that give teachers a great deal of discretion, particularly over classroom matters. It is important for teachers to fully understand this cellular characteristic, because it represents a trade-off, a sacrifice of power at higher levels, and is one key to the amount of discretion, or options, available to them.

Lortie makes no explicit value judgment about structural looseness. It might produce inefficiency in some types of organizations, in which the production process is linear, programmed and predictable. However, it can be useful, even essential, in human service organizations with less precise technologies and less predictable outcomes. Given that learning is an imprecise process, structural looseness may help to assure that individual differences will be handled.

Lortie's conclusion about the amount of discretion that teachers do have may seem to differ from Hottleman's views, but their differences can be easily explained. Lortie is talking about the amount of discretion that individual teachers have within their classrooms. He concludes that they do have a great deal of discretion. In contrast, Hottleman is concerned about the collective power of teachers to influence larger issues extending beyond individual classrooms. He contends that individual teachers do not have much power at that level. These two conclusions are consistent with our discussion of power and autonomy in Volume I and in Part I of this volume: Autonomy does not bestow power. Indeed, often employees are permitted to exercise discretion over minor matters only because they do not have the power to effect the important outcomes. For this reason, it is always important before taking action to consider the degree to which larger issues influence the smaller context.

COPING STRATEGIES

Given these differences in approaches to and views of organizations, it is understandable that the authors propose different strategies for coping with organizations. The term "coping strategies" refers here to the individual or collective means that people use to achieve their personal goals, whether the goal is to survive, to succeed, to exercise influence, or whatever.

Tumin suggests some very specific coping strategies individuals may use. His rules, aimed primarily at new teachers, indicate how "ritualistic conformity," as it was referred to in Volume I can be adopted to advantage. The purpose of rules is to help the individual succeed in schools as they currently operate. Individuals, of course, can choose not to follow rules, but at great risk to their prospects for achieving success within the organization.

Tumin's discussion serves a useful purpose beyond providing guidance to those who choose to follow it. For the rules, almost cynically, clarify what it can cost an individual to "survive" in terms of his or her self-concept, integrity, initiative and esteem. Put in these stark terms, some readers may decide that survival is not enough.

Hottleman proposes activism as a different coping strategy. (We referred to this as the "rebellious" strategy in Volume I.) His advice is directed to individuals as a collective response. It is possible for teachers to follow Tumin's rules when responding individually and Hottleman's advice when responding collectively. What Hottleman proposes has in fact been a prevalent response of both the NEA and the AFT in recent years. However, as Lortie suggests, effective use of this strategy requires more sophisticated knowledge about organization than many teachers can now claim.

A somewhat more analytical approach is suggested in Lortie's discussion. He does not prescribe specific coping strategies. He prognosticates. He predicts some future developments, based on projections of current trends and his obvious familiarity with teaching. He invites the reader to analyze the conditions and circumstances and to reach his or her own conclusions. However, his remarks suggest that improved technology, and research and development can help individuals better deal with organizations, and can help teachers deal with the future by anticipating the trends and understanding the reasons for them. He seems to be saying that one can cope better with an organization if one pauses to analyze it. This step introduces the notion of an organizational ecology and is advisable before one adopts any mode of coping.

In view of the interdependence of organizational characteristics it can be expected that if power changes, other things will change as well. Recognizing this, Lortie suggests at least one important change to accompany increased teacher power. Power has a price: teachers will be held more accountable for the failures and the successes of schools as they enter more fully into decision making.

The fact that each author seems to be thinking of the different costs and rewards for teachers helps explain why they chose to concentrate on different coping strategies. Tumin is being realistic and careful about the risks involved for new teachers who ignore the power structure of education. Hottleman, on the other hand, stresses the need for change and the possible gains that could occur from collective action, not only because there are fewer risks in collective action, but also because he is being more visionary about how teaching should be. But we suspect all of the writers would agree that no one coping strategy is sufficient. A variety of coping strategies is useful, depending upon the circumstances. Timing is especially important. For example, Tumin's recommendations are aimed at new teachers before they have experience and tenure. Both experience and tenure can reduce the risk or provide some of the wisdom and job security a person needs to act in innovative ways. Under some conditions, rebellion can be seen as a prelude to innovation or an alternative to it or perhaps complementary to it. Finally, we should note that the effectiveness of a strategy depends in part upon the era and social reward. Rebellion, innovation, and retreat seem to have been more characteristic of some decades than of others in recent times.

THE ROLE OF CONFLICT

All three authors believe that organizational conflict is normal and often useful. For Lortie, it is inherent in the fact that authority is problematic. For Tumin, it is promoted by vague or inconsistent goals and success criteria, and the heterogeneity of the clientele. Hottleman evaluates conflict to the status of one of his two major purposes of organization. It is particularly interesting that from very divergent evolutionary, pragmatic, and advocacy positions, Tumin, Lortie and Hottleman all reach the same conclusion: that collective bargaining potentially can make a positive contribution to education.

As the three authors suggest, conflict is probably produced by the division of labor, and also by the fact that employees have different goals and allegiances to a variety of people outside of the organization. We might also add that employees who have direct contact with the clientele outside the organization (who are unlikely to be committed to organizational norms) will be under special pressure to deviate. Conflict between these individuals and employees who do not have to cope with these conflicting pressures is probably as important as the line and staff tensions that Lortie mentions.

One value of Hottleman's discussion is that it highlights the positive contribution that conflict can make to improving organizations, both as a means of forcing change and of compromise. Conflict serves to challenge assumptions and stretch thinking, to create discomfort with existing practices, and even to threaten the parties involved, thus prompting them to entertain changes. Once these functions of conflict have been recognized, it is important to begin to synthesize the conflict perspective with other organization perspectives.

People come to very different conclusions about how useful, or "functional" conflict is, depending upon (a) whether their purpose is to improve coordination or to permit wider participation in setting goals, (b) the type of organization they have in mind, and (c) the degree of conflict they are considering. On the first point, while conflict is probably necessary for the process of goal setting, continuing, major conflicts can hinder coordination. It is the price of a participatory democracy, and part of the trade-off between the effectiveness and efficiency of organizations. On the second point, conflict is more central to some organizations than to others and so can be more easily accommodated in some than in others. Labor unions, perhaps, are formed specifically to carry on conflict, but many organizations exist for purely social reasons. Finally, we should remember that while power can be used for good, like any other tool it can also be destructive unless effective conflict resolution mechanisms are available. But if conflict can be resolved, even partially, it can be a vital stimulus for improvement.

PARTICIPATION IN DECISIONS

All of the authors believe that hierarchy is a central feature of schools, but they differ on whether it is inevitable and on who can participate in the key decisions. One of the central issues concerns the extent to which people in the hierarchy take into account various constituencies and, more important, the opportunities for these constituencies to share in the decisions. Lortie and Tumin seem to see far more groups participating than does Hottleman. The same rationale and strategies that Hottleman advocates could easily be extended to students. Teachers pitted against their students is an eventuality that he does not, nor was he asked to, consider.

COMPARISONS BETWEEN SCHOOLS AND OTHER ORGANIZATIONS

There are many reasonable ways in which organizations can be compared, for example: the control employees have over their daily schedules; the criteria used to determine the client's eligibility to receive services offered by the organization; the amount of incentive for employees to be responsive to the needs and desires of different categories of clients; and the extent to which employees and laymen participate in the control of the organization. The reader probably can think of still other salient dimensions.

Both Lortie and Tumin identify a few of these ways in which schools differ from other types of organizations. They recognize that schools render a service to the public, are publicly and locally controlled, operate on conflicting criteria of success, rely on compulsory attendance and on standardized technology. The fact that schools are the only major social service on which citizens vote directly and frequently is another important difference, which seriously interferes with continuity and planning but which also gives the public some voice in educational policy.

It is important to consider such differences, as well as the similarities, because teachers could get a jaundiced, parochial view of their world if not exposed to other modes of work. Unless teachers make a deliberate effort to maintain perspective, they can become molded simply by the pressures of being treated in certain ways for long periods of time, and thus come to think of themselves in an isolated role. Persons could become different from what they could have been because the organization was allowed to shape the individual. Some influence, i.e., "being socialized," is inevitable, but the teacher who maintains some perspective on the larger world of organizations can remain a broader person.

THE SIGNIFICANCE OF ORGANIZATIONAL THEORY

All three writers are convinced that organizational theory can be useful to teachers and other citizens. If Tumin is correct in his claim that large school organization is here to stay, all of us will either have to learn to live more effectively with it or discover more than is now known about how to decentralize more effectively and organize in other ways. Hottleman sees knowledge about organizations and organizing as an effective approach for individuals who do not have much power. And Lortie is persuasive when he predicts that organizations will become more technologically complex. If Lortie's predictions about the new school technology prove true, teachers will no longer be able to isolate themselves from the events of the larger school and school district. They will have to develop a much larger perspective, become prepared for an increasing scope of responsibilities, and gain the skills to interact with many more colleagues in a more complex environment.

CONCLUSION

While the authors represent different persuasions that for argument's sake provide valid contrasts, one should be careful not to overgeneralize about an author's position. Due to space limitations, each author has been able to present only a partial treatment. What is important for our purposes is that there are many valid approaches to the study of organizations which, though at times controversial or confusing, can in

78

combination help an interested person arrive at a more comprehensive view of the organizations to which he or she belongs.

SOME QUESTIONS FOR DISCUSSION

Before turning to some additional considerations not yet fully dealt with, we want to urge each reader to reflect further on these papers. They are rich in insight, but we have only begun to touch upon their full implications. Rather than try to summarize at this point, we would rather conclude our discussion with a series of questions:

1. Contrast Hottleman's discussion of hierarchy with that of Tumin and Lortie. Is there an absolute need for hierarchy in the organization of the school? If so, how can it be justified? What should its function be? How can teachers exert influence to assure that the negative aspects of hierarchy are minimized or reduced? Are there alternatives to hierarchy? What might they be?

2. Can a person at the top of the hierarchy long continue to wield power unfairly, indiscriminately, against the will of the majority in a school organization? How can teachers check the misuse of power?

3. Compare Hottleman's and Lortie's points of view on conflict. Which seems more valid to you? Are there other views on conflict that should be considered?

4. Is there any position between Tumin (in his rules) and Hottleman, as an activist, that more appropriately serves your purpose?

5. Contrast Lortie's discussion of technology with Tumin's.

6. Which of the authors seems to be most familiar with the teaching profession? Which seems to view it from an outside or neutral position? How important is it to be able to view teaching and the school objectively as a social system?

7. Contrast Tumin's perspective of organizational intent with Hottleman's.

8. Compare and evaluate the ways Tumin and Lortie indicate that schools differ from other formal organizations.

9. Are Tumin's rules directed more at individual behavior or at organizational phenomenon? Would these rules apply equally well to college professors? To self-employed business persons? To corporation executives?

10. It seems obvious that the authors are suggesting or inferring that schools need to be reorganized. That might mean decentralization, reducing hierarchy, etc. Looking at your own school, what reform or reorganization would contribute to improvement?

Part III

Schools and Teachers in Action

Part I of this book describes some characteristics of schools as social organizations and raises issues surrounding the complexity of defining schools and comparing one school with another. In Part II, Dan Lortie, Melvin Tumin, and Girard Hottleman use their own approaches in addressing teachers about schools as organizations, and Roy Edelfelt and Ronald Corwin present their reflections on the three discussions. The purpose of this section is to describe some possible activities that might help participants explore the issues in Parts I and II and test and apply concepts raised by the authors. A summary of the activities is followed by suggested procedures and other information needed to carry out each exercise.

The instructor should select activities in the order that best suits participant levels of awareness and the instructional purpose. Participants or instructors will probably want to modify or add to the list of activities offered.

Summary of Activities
1. Draw a School. An introductory exercise.
2. Schools as Organizations. Reading about and discussing schools.
3. John Banks. Using a case study to apply what has been learned about schools.
4. Writing a Case Study. Relating an understanding of schools as organizations to personal experience.
5. *Up the Down Staircase.* Applying what has been learned to a feature length film.

Activity 1
Draw a School

The purpose of this activity is to assist participants as they continue to refine their understandings of schools. After reading Part I of this volume, "Schools: A Kaleidoscopic View," participants are encouraged to consider the schools where they are or have been employed and to illustrate graphically the organizations as they view them. Consideration of the following steps may be helpful:

- Draw the school you have been considering. (The instructor should provide chart paper and marking pens.) Use pictures, words or symbols if you like. Do not draw an organization chart. Do try to include what you feel are important elements of the school organization. (10 minutes)
- Show your drawing to others in the group. Explain what the drawing depicts. Group members may ask questions to help you further define the characteristics of the school you have described. (Five minutes for each participant)
- Review the drawings of each group member and compare or contrast the characteristics they have illustrated. Consider likenesses and differences such as
  — complexity of the organization
  — hierarchy
  — locus of power, authority
  — communications systems
  — decision-making systems
  — goals
  — autonomy
  — status
  — formal and informal procedures
  — rules and regulations
  — boundaries: who is inside, who is outside?
  — etc.*

Participants may proceed next to the reading of Part II. They will have the opportunity to relate their views of schools to the views of three authors, Dan Lortie, Melvin Tumin, and Girard Hottleman.

---

*A list of concepts that may apply to the discussion is contained in Volume I, page 47.

Activity 2

Schools as Organizations

Participants begin their reading of Part II, "Schools as Organizations: Three Discussions with Commentary," with the understanding that schools are complex organizations that can be viewed from various vantage points. The papers contained in Part II should provoke enthusiastic discussion.

The instructor might employ a presentation and debate strategy to capitalize on the participants' reactions to the papers. A description of that strategy follows.

- Divide participants into three groups and assign one paper (Lortie, Tumin, or Hottleman) to each group.
- Instruct the groups to read their papers and prepare a five minute overview of the paper for the whole group.
- Instruct the groups to develop a critique of the papers using some questions such as the following as a guide:
  —What issues does the author want the reader to consider?
  —On which characteristics of schools as organizations does the author focus?
  —With which points do you agree, disagree, take issue, feel challenged?
  —How might teachers begin to utilize or apply concepts presented in the paper?
  —What cautions or advice would you give to another teacher reading this paper?
- Ask each group to present the overview of its paper to the whole group, then open the session to discussion using the above questions as a guide.
- Have participants read papers they have not read.
- Summarize the session and suggest that participants study Part II, Section 4, "Some Reflections on Issues Raised in the Three Discussions." Written by Roy Edelfelt and Ronald Corwin, the article provides yet another viewpoint on the Lortie, Tumin, and Hottleman papers. Additional questions for discussion appear at the end of the article.

Activity 3

John Banks: A Sequential Case Study

The intent of this case study is to present an existing problem situation and develop an explanation and analysis based upon identifying relevant organizational characteristics and norms.

The analysis focuses, in part, on the positions of the major players in the organizational hierarchy with additional emphasis given to the phenomena of conflict, power, authority, and autonomy. The vulnerability of the school organization based upon its environmental context is also addressed.

The case selected for discussion here has been included for illustrative purposes. It is not necessarily the only case that can be used, and the reader may wish to find or write others that are more appropriate. (See Activity 4.) Nor is there any one correct interpretation; each analyst will bring a personal perspective. What is important is that in the process of reflecting on a case, abstract concepts and ideas take on additional dimensions of meaning and significance.

SUGGESTIONS FOR USE OF CASE

"John Banks" is a case study that gives the reader an excellent opportunity to identify characteristics of organizations and organizational norms and to examine role conflicts and coping strategies.

The case is sequential and contains three parts (A, B, and C) which may be read and discussed separately. The sequential approach allows participants to consider small amounts of information at a time. Some ways in which the case may be used are suggested below. The suggestions are followed by a copy of the case study and by an analysis of the case.

- The instructor might begin by reviewing the case study and the analysis in order to plan its introduction to participants and to plan the discussions that will follow each part of the case. If possible, we suggest that discussions be in small groups of 8-12 people. Participants should know that the case represents one technique for applying the knowledge they have been acquiring. They should be encouraged to examine John's problem from an organizational and a personal point of view.

- The following procedure is one way to work through the case.

    1. Distribute Part A. Read, discuss and identify the possible conflicts that might occur.

2. Distribute Part B. (You may wish to have participants read A and B before beginning any discussion.) The following questions might be posed:
   —How would you describe the problem in this case? What organizational characteristics are contributing to it?
   —In what ways could this problem best be dealt with?
   —What would you do in this situation if you were John? If you were the principal? Why?
   —What are the sources of pressure acting on the individuals and groups in this case?
   —What organizational norms are in play?

3. Distribute Part C. Read and discuss, using the following questions as a guide:
   —Does your analysis of the situation change with the additional information? How?
   —What organizational characteristics are contributing to the problem?
   —What strategies could John use to cope with the problem? What would you do now?
   —If "John" Banks had been a woman rather than a man, would it have made any difference in your analysis of the case? If so, why?

4. Summarize the case.

• Additional suggestions for the use of the case would be to have the participants role play conversations between the teacher and the principal. In one case, the teacher could role play an individual following Tumin's advice. In another situation the teacher could model his or her behavior upon the suggestions of Hottleman. Participants could be asked to analyze the outcomes of both types of behavior.

To achieve some measure of closure, it will be important to generalize about the analysis of the case. Organizational characteristics considered during the analysis should be emphasized. Questions such as the following may assist in summarizing the case.

• What parallels do you see between this case and the Terry Trevors case presented in Volume I, and the film recommended for this volume, *Up the Down Staircase*? For example, what is the relative importance of the bureaucracy and the community as a source of control in each situation? What are the major differences in the problems of each case?

• What would you do if you were in John Bank's place? If you were a friend or colleague what advice would you give to him?

- Can you see ways in which Tumin's recommendations apply or do not apply in this case?
- What implications does Lortie's analysis of the classroom autonomy of teachers have for this case?
- Could Hottleman's analyses and prescriptions apply to this case? Why or why not?

MAJOR CONCEPTS

- Organizational Models
  Rational Model
  Organic Model
- Formal Organization
- Informal Organization
- Formal Group
- Informal Group
- Autonomy
  Insulation
  Isolation
  Discretion
  Interdependence
- Zones of Autonomy
- Organizational Hierarchy
  Employee
  Subordinate
  Superordinate
- Expertise

- Status Inconsistency
- Control Mechanisms
  Power
  Authority
  Cooptation
  Coercion
- Mutual Runner
- Collegial Solidarity
- Environment
  External Environment
  Stable Environment
- Alienation
- Professional Teaching Norms
- Community Institution
- Conflict
- Hierarchy
- Range, position
- Coping strategies

MAJOR CHARACTERS

- John Banks—An untenured, second year, sixth grade teacher
- Sara Flowers—An elementary principal

ORGANIZATIONS AND GROUPS

- Faculty of Magnolia Elementary School
- Shelbyville City School System
- Shelbyville Teachers Association (STA)
- National Education Association (NEA)
- State Affiliate of NEA
- The Shelbyville community

THE CASE IN BRIEF

John Banks is a sixth grade teacher who is primarily interested in social studies. He is in his second year of teaching and is untenured. In his spare time John enjoys operating a small farm in the southern community in which he lives. After his first year of teaching, John decides to concentrate on strengthening and improving the social studies component of his next sixth grade class. He subsequently chooses to use part of the *Man: A Course of Study* (MACOS), curriculum, but falls victim to an unexpected result. The mother of one of his pupils complains to and threatens Ms. Flowers, the school principal, regarding the content and values she perceives him to be teaching. The events that follow lead to conflict between John and Ms. Flowers. Ms. Flowers "requests" that John discontinue his use of MACOS and stay within the parameters of the adopted text. The local superintendent is campaigning for state superintendent of public instruction. John perceives Ms. Flowers to be evading her professional responsibilities for, among other reasons, political expediency. Even though she reminds him that he is on a year-to-year contract and that compromises are sometimes necessary, John is determined not to comply without pursuing the matter further.

John Banks: Sixth Grade Teacher

by Mark Newton

Part A

John Banks graduated summa cum laude from one of the "Big Ten" universities in the Northeastern United States. He majored in elementary education and took an additional area of concentration in anthropology. John's desire, following graduation, was to return to his home state, located well below the Mason-Dixon line. He wanted to teach in or near a rural community so that he could build and operate a small farm in his free time—something he had always wanted to do.

John's collegiate recommendations were impeccable. His major advisor in college (who was also his supervising teacher during his student teaching experience) indicated that . . . "John possesses the raw qualities of a humanistic master teacher and displays many attributes of effective democratic leadership."

During his senior year, John was interviewed at the university by recruiters from a number of large southern school systems. The recruiters were impressed with him and most of them requested that his credentials be sent to their respective central offices. But John really preferred a small school system in a rural area.

Since recruiters from small school systems in the south did not typically recruit at the university John attended, John sent his resume and transcript to a number of such systems in his home state. After several weeks he was invited to interview with the superintendents of two of the systems. Following the interviews, he was offered a position in both systems. John selected the Shelbyville school system because he felt it to be most consistent with his personal and professional needs and desires. His appointment, however, was contigent upon his completing two additional courses required for elementary certification by his state. John's intent was to complete the courses during the summer following his graduation.

During the summer as he worked toward completion of the courses necessary for certification, John again met with Dr. Lazarus, the superintendent. Also sitting in were the principals of three of the elementary schools in the system. As a result of the meeting, John was officially appointed to Magnolia Elementary School as a sixth grade teacher where the principal would be Ms. Sara Flowers. She had been present at the summer interview and was very congenial.

Ms. Flowers is a native of the Shelbyville community. A woman in her mid-fifties, she had been a teacher in the Shelbyville system for twenty years before assuming a principalship. She is the only woman administrator in the system. Her husband is an executive in Shelbyville's largest bank, and has recently served as a special budgetary advisor to the governor.

Shelbyville is the county seat of Warren County. The population of 20,000 is known, statewide, for its political and social conservatism. (It voted dry in 1952 and remains dry today.) Most of the residents are engaged in small acreage crop farming while simultaneously working in local industrial plants as semiskilled production employees, or are associated with the town's small business sector.

The religious orientation of the community is predominately fundamentalist. A large segment of the city and county population attends ultra-right wing splinter churches that have broken away from established conservative Protestant denominations.

The majority of teachers and administrators in the schools are graduates of the same regional university, located forty miles away. John is part of the forty-five percent who has not graduated from that university and one of a very few who has not graduated from an instate institution.

John thoroughly enjoys his first year of teaching. He is an automatic hit with the youngsters, especially the older boys—he is one of two males on a teaching staff of 18. Such a disproportionate ratio creates no real problems for John. He has established good rapport with both his colleagues and Ms. Flowers and has met with minimal peer criticism or advice regarding innovative teaching methodologies and/or curriculum materials he experiments with during that first year.

At times, however, John feels somewhat isolated from his professional colleagues. Most of them belong to various formal and informal groups defined by sex. Their group activities or concerns are often the topics of their conversations in the teachers' lounge and in the halls. Consequently, John often finds himself either disinterested or unable to relate. He has, however, joined the Shelbyville Teachers Association (STA) in an attempt to establish professional male friendships, but attends meetings irregularly. Most of his spare time is spent working on a small farm he has acquired.

The STA is a small group of teachers. It primarily represents the junior and senior high school levels. The members have the reputation in the school system of being the most vocal advocates for collective bargaining and generally are the most liberal. Few elementary teachers belong. John also holds membership in his state's affiliate of the NEA, as well as NEA itself.

John Banks: A Sixth Grade Teacher — Part B

The summer following his first year of teaching, John begins working toward a Master's degree at the nearby university. During that time he becomes acquainted with the ESEA Title III Materials Resource Center (MRC) and its holdings. The MRC is housed in the college of education at the university. John's school system is located in the geographic region that is able to utilize materials and services of the MRC.

One afternoon, as John browses through some shelves at the MRC, he uncovers a complete upper elementary social studies curriculum, *Man: A Course of Study* (MACOS), that he studied and respected as an undergraduate. John had previously requested that MACOS be ordered at the local level but had been told that the cost was prohibitive in terms of existing funds for curriculum materials.

The MACOS materials at the MRC are still boxed and unused. John is excitedly aware that the entire curriculum is available for his use through the regional MRC.

As the summer passes, John begins developing curricula and toying with ideas for his next sixth grade class. He feels that he is able to devote more time to curriculum and instruction this year than he has during his first year because he has learned the non-instructional procedures and mechanics unique to his school and system during his first year.

John has both a personal and professional interest in anthropology and history (and social studies in general). He has an intense desire to build a stronger social studies component in his sixth grade classes. Consequently, John decides that, as part of their study of other cultures, his students will study the Netsilik Eskimos, a unit in the MACOS curriculum.

It is John's intent to "introduce his youngsters to the Netsilik Eskimos so they will understand and appreciate people of different cultures and thereby better understand themselves." John chooses MACOS, not only because he is familiar with it or for its fine professional reputation, but also because its themes and content are drawn from anthropology, social psychology, and biology—areas that greatly interest him.

School opens in September. In November, John's class begins to study the Netsilik Eskimos in depth. His students are intrigued by and enamored with the curriculum materials, especially the movies that are real ethnographic records.

Toward the mid-point of studying the Netsilik Eskimos, Ms. Flowers visits John's classroom twice in a one week period. This occurrence seems unusual to John as Ms. Flowers has only visited his class once before—almost a year ago, when he first began teaching.

One day, the following week, Ms. Flowers asks John to stop by her office before leaving for the day. At that meeting, she informs John that she has received a serious complaint from the mother of one of his pupils. The nature of the complaint concerns the content associated with studying the Netsilik Eskimos.

Ms. Flowers indicates that the mother is irate because "Mr. Banks is teaching our children about wife swapping; he's teaching that wife swapping is not a sin; and he's instilling other immoral ideas in their heads." The mother (according to Ms. Flowers) further states that "If you (Ms. Flowers) don't see that he ceases this immediately, I'm going to assemble all the parents of the students in the class and make sure they know the kind of stuff that that man is teaching."

At first John is shocked at the accusation levied against him. He informs Ms. Flowers that the situation was an "absurdity" and that it was "an example of what takes place when a parent doesn't visit the school, but makes assumptions from bits and pieces of information relayed by her or the neighbor's children."

Ms. Flowers asks John where there could possibly be an association between wife swapping and his social studies units. Further, she indicates that when she visited his class the previous week, she, frankly, had been impressed with the student's "level of discussion" concerning the Eskimos and their obvious interest, but found nothing "out of order" regarding content.

John answers by relating a situation that is part of the Netsilik Eskimo unit. The situation concerns the ill wife of one of the Eskimo hunters. Due to her illness, the wife is unable to make a long, arduous,

90

and cold journey to the hunting areas which are miles away. Consequently, the hunter, through mutual agreement, borrows the physically able wife of one of his friends. His friend, therefore, agrees to care for the hunter's ill wife until the journey is over.

Wives in the Netsilik culture play an important role relative to such journeys. They prepare food for the hunters after each day's hunt; maintain the base camps as the hunters move from hunt site to hunt site; skin the felled game and prepare it for preservation; assist in carrying supplies; and provide needed body warmth to the hunters (typically their husbands) during the bitter cold nights. Such "borrowing" arrangements are common and necessary in the Netsilik Eskimo culture.

John discusses with Ms. Flowers how he feels that such true anthropological accounts provide students with a basis for comparing, through discussion and writing, different cultures, different human behavioral patterns, and different human relationships drawn from "the real world." He further relates how MACOS has received national recognition as a breakthrough in the elementary social studies curriculum; that it has been developed by the prestigious Jerome Bruner and his Harvard associates; that it has been funded by both the National Science Foundation, as well as the Ford Foundation; and that it is used and recommended by many school systems across the country.

Ms. Flowers thanks John for his time and information and tells him she will give the matter more detailed consideration and meet with him again soon. She indicates that her main concern is maintaining harmony.

John Banks: Sixth Grade Teacher — Part C

Two days later Ms. Flowers again asks John to stop by her office. At the end of the day, he complies with the request.

Ms. Flowers tells John she has given their mutual concern considerable attention and wishes to make two points. She states:

> First, John, this is a conservative Baptist community. Consequently, you must be overly sensitive to the substantive content you bring before your classroom. Things that seem innocent and educational to you and me often receive negative reactions here.

> Secondly, Dr. Lazarus is a pretty good bet for the next state superintendent of public instruction, and he's campaigning hard for it. I don't think it would be wise to stir up something locally that could hinder his chances of being elected.

John asks Ms. Flowers if she really means that he should discontinue the present study and any further study of the Netsilik Eskimos. She replies that she feels that it would be best, at least for the present time, if "you don't use any of the MACOS curriculum and stay within the parameters of the system's adopted sixth grade social studies text."

John is angered at this "suggestion" and asks if he might conduct a parent awareness program regarding the entire sequence of units in the MACOS curriculum. He further asks Ms. Flowers if she is really familiar with MACOS. Her only response is that "we don't want a Kanawha County, West Virginia situation here."

John then becomes overtly critical of what he perceives to be occurring. He asks Ms. Flowers:

> Are you *telling* me that I am restricted to the topics addressed in a text that was adopted seven years ago; a text that I feel stresses blind acceptance, the status quo, and caution—simply because one parent misunderstands one small facet of an entire social studies curriculum?
>
> If that is, indeed, what you are saying, then you are evading your responsibility to me as my principal.

In response to that remark, Ms. Flowers adds an additional caution to the previous two. She states in a curt tone:

> I am not *telling* you you must stay within the topical areas of the adopted text. I am not *telling* you you may not utilize MACOS, but I am reminding you that you are still on a year-to-year contract. As you know, tenure is not considered here until the fourth year. I suggest you give some thought to that, John.
>
> I want us to work in harmony with one another, with the central office, and the community. You should realize that compromises are sometimes necessary. I've been here all my life and, John, I know when those compromises are necessary. This is one of those times. The parent who called me exerts a considerable amount of influence with other parents. No matter how good MACOS is, or how recognized its developers, that particular mother will see and hear only what she wants to see and hear. That means trouble for us all.
>
> Additionally, Dr. Lazarus has worked long and hard here. He deserves this chance to go to the capital where he can do good for all of us. He shouldn't have to wrestle with a potential problem like this with the election so close.

John leaves Ms. Flowers' office angered and confused. He needs time to think through his complete course of action, but one thing he is sure of—an authority higher than his building principal will have to request his discontinuance of *Man: A Course of Study* before he will consider abandoning it in his classroom.

John Banks: Sixth Grade Teacher—

An Analysis by Mark Newton

The preceding case study portrays a problem ignited by a parent of one of John Bank's sixth grade pupils. Any analysis of the case must consider John Banks, Ms. Flowers, and the organizational and community characteristics that bear on the events.

ORGANIC VS. RATIONAL MODEL

From the limited amount of data presented, one is hard pressed to label Magnolia Elementary School as clearly "rational" or "organic" in nature—or to study it solely from one of the two perspectives. Certainly, illustrations of both models can be found in the school and/or school system. However, from the organizational characteristics presented, it appears that Magnolia Elementary School is operating in ways consistent with the organic model.

Several elements of an organic model are evident. First, there is not necessarily a one-to-one relationship between authority (as vested in Ms. Flowers) and expertise.

Expertise implies know-how or requisite technical knowledge. Ms. Flowers' authority is not debatable. Her title and role give legitimacy to her authority. However, the degree to which she exercised administrative expertise in dealing with the problem at hand is debatable. Keeping the parent's complaint from John for over a week while observing him, failing to support him against a disgruntled parent, failing to discuss the entire situation and extenuating circumstances with John in depth, and threatening his future employment status in the school system all cast doubt on her administrative skill. Further, her position as principal, may have been a reward for loyalty or for years of service rather than a result of administrative potential or expertise.

Secondly, Ms. Flowers tries to employ compromise to resolve conflict. "You should realize that compromises are sometimes necessary . . . This is one of those times," she informs John. Also, consistent with organic assumptions, survival needs are salient when Ms. Flowers indicates she is attempting to avoid another "Kanawha County, West Virginia situation" rather than address the academic freedom or curricular discretion of John Banks, or reassess any existing articulated goals/objectives of the school's social studies curriculum, or study the MACOS curriculum in enough detail to determine its merit or drawbacks relative to the immediate internal and external social, political, moral, and educational milieus.

Additionally, in Ms. Flowers' opinion, the maintenance of the status quo, so that Dr. Lazarus could campaign without turmoil at home, takes precedence over other more official goals. This points to the utilization of situational supervision by Ms. Flowers. The insulation and isolation initially enjoyed by John is diminished following the parent's complaint.

The "organic" nature of what is known about Magnolia Elementary School has been depicted in order to contrast it with the corresponding "rational" characteristics: authority backed with corresponding level of expertise, articulated and understood goals, and close coordination. These characteristics are not in evidence from the data presented.

The ability to recognize the presence or absence of these and other characteristics should prove fruitful for interpreting and understanding organizational characteristics as well as for developing alternatives for dealing with identifiable problems. If one is inclined to bring about organizational change or improvement and chooses to work within "the system," an understanding of and appreciation for organizational characteristics will facilitate that endeavor.

HIERARCHY

Other organizational variables can be identified by assessing the positions of John Banks and Ms. Flowers in the organizational hierarchy. John Banks is employed as a sixth grade teacher at Magnolia Elementary School. The fact that he is an employee denotes that he is a subordinate in a hierarchy. Consequently, a formal superordinate/subordinate relationship exists between Ms. Flowers and John. No matter what the technical or professional expertise of Ms. Flowers (be it greater than, equal to, or less than that of John Banks) she, by position in the hierarchy, possesses formal and official authority. John's authority is restricted to the classroom.

This superordinate/subordinate relationship between Ms. Flowers and John appears to be dominative in nature, supporting the often held contention that the authority of school administrators over teachers is primarily dominative. This dominance is, in part, a response to the necessity of mediating demands of local citizens. However, John Banks does not perceive Ms. Flowers as a mediator of community demands. He sees her as an administrator who fails to protect him from the demands of an angry parent and who places a higher premium on public relations and the political environment than on instructional/curricular quality or professional responsibility.

Indeed, Ms. Flowers is forced to choose between sound professional judgment and political expediency. She opts for political expediency. Sound professional judgment might lead to a more indepth and objective assessment of the problem situation than is given by Ms. Flowers. Potential alternatives and their ramifications might be explored jointly by John, Ms. Flowers and, eventually, Dr. Lazarus. In all probability, other personnel, both internal and external to the school (including the board), might be involved. This process, in Ms. Flowers' opinion, would be unpleasant and has the potential for severely hindering Dr. Lazarus' chances of obtaining state level office. Additionally, Ms. Flowers stands the chance of blemishing both her and her husband's professional and social standing in the community. Going the politically expedient route, then, seems to Ms. Flowers, the safest approach.

AUTHORITY

John, like most teachers, accepts the official authority of the principal in pupil-parent relations but questions the right of a principal to dictate matters related to curriculum and instruction. To John, Ms. Flowers should function as a colleague whose supervision of curriculum and instruction is based on professional competence, and who renders constructive criticism rather than subtle mandates. He fails to recognize or accept some of the real variables that affect her administrative domain—many of which relate directly or indirectly to the external political arena, and which may have impact on the school itself in the final analysis.

John is reacting to what he has been socialized ideally to expect. The opposite has occurred. Ms. Flowers chooses not to protect his academic freedom, or his autonomy. She chooses, rather, to exercise her authority over curricular matters in favor of the parent, Dr. Lazarus, and perhaps herself. Some sociological investigations report that a general conflict in school organizations exists because teachers assume a professional status while simultaneously functioning as subordinates in the hierarchy. This phenomenon appears consistent with the situation in the case study.

Even though a professional, John is almost powerless by virtue of his hierarchical position and the short period of time he has held that position. Consequently, from a hierarchical perspective John is responsible for carrying out Ms. Flowers' policies or "suggestions" and, accordingly, is subject to her evaluations of his professional competence. As a teacher, he is officially without legitimate power or authority outside the classroom. The maximum negative sanction, dismissal, used primarily with untenured teachers, is a potential consequence if he chooses non-compliance as a viable alternative. Ms. Flowers points that out to John when she reminds him that he is still on a "year-to-year contract."

POWER

Does John have any power at all? If so, what are the sources of his power? Yes, John has power if he chooses to exercise it. He has power on the grounds that he considers himself to be a professional and to be one who possesses a sense of what is professionally ethical and right. However, he needs support, and the consequences of attempting to secure it must be weighed.

Where might John find backing? One alternative for John is to secure legal assistance, and if necessary, take the situation into a court of law. A court would probably render a favorable decision. But what would happen then? Would the end justify the means? Would he be employed in an environment where he is relatively unwanted or psychologically ostracized? Would he become ineffective or be forced into ineffectiveness? Would he be able to make a difference? The ultimate question in considering the merits and worth of taking and standing by a position is: When does it pay to fight the organization? Each individual must answer the question for him—or herself.

As another alternative, possibly the Shelbyville Teachers Association, or the state affiliate of NEA can exert enough pressure to protect his viewpoint if they are so inclined. For tenured teachers, the claim of professional status offers some power-related advantages. Such status typically denotes a certain amount of collegial solidarity. John, however, feels rather isolated from the majority of teaching staff at Magnolia. He is one of only two males on the staff and indicates that he can't relate to the teachers' lounge and hall conservations which, apparently, are often unrelated to the professional norms of teaching. Additionally, from what is presented about the community, it is probably safe to assume that the majority of the elementary teachers in the system are not alienated from the community to the degree many teachers are in many communities. Most belong to out-of-school formal and informal groups and few belong to the local teachers' organization. What effect would a weak teachers' organization have on John's situation? What about the fact that most of the teachers belong to external groups defined by sex and that John is one of only two males on the school's teaching staff?

Further, John's association with teachers in other buildings is minimal. The case study indicates that he spends most of his free time developing his newly acquired farm and attends meetings of the Shelbyville Teachers Association rather infrequently. Will this inhibit his chances of obtaining collegial or professional support among his colleagues system wide relative to the problem he faces?

If the Shelbyville Teachers Association is, indeed, a solid group of the more liberal and vocal teachers in the system, some influence on Ms. Flowers and/or other appropriate administrators will probably be a real possibility, if it is mustered.

RANK AND POSITION

From the data presented in the case study, what positions does John hold and what are the circumstances around those positions? Three positions are salient. John is:

- an untenured sixth grade teacher with slightly more than one year of teaching experience;
- a member, but infrequent attendee, of the Shelbyville Teachers' Organization;
- a member of the National Education Association (which includes membership in the state affiliate).

These positions probably do not offer John much protection. However, it is reasonable to speculate that, of the three positions, membership in the Shelbyville Teachers' Organization could potentially offer the most protection and exert the greatest influence on the administration. The organization must, however, be strong and persistent if it is to be of value to John. If it is weak, its support may do him harm.

John is at a further power disadvantage because he has established few community ties. He has lived in the Shelbyville area for less than two years. Additionally, his collegiate socialization differs from the majority of his peers and colleagues, both within and across the system. The case study indicates that only a few of the system's teachers possess degrees from outside the state. But John is not a complete alien, the state in which he is teaching is his home state.

Now consider Sara Flowers in a bit more detail. Ms. Flowers holds the bureaucratic position of principal of one of Shelbyville City School System's subunits—Magnolia Elementary School. As principal, she is the immediate superordinate of 18 elementary teachers. This position automatically places her at a power advantage relative to those teachers, especially untenured teachers like John Banks.

As principal, Ms. Flowers is also responsible for fulfilling official policy as directed by the superintendent. Additionally, she is most likely constrained to meet certain informal or unofficial expectations of the superintendent. Those expectations could well include such things as aligning herself with his philosophical orientation, agreeing with or acting on her perceptions of his priorities (i.e., student control vs. student autonomy, or teacher control vs. teacher autonomy, etc.), assisting with his campaign for chief state school officer by exerting influence where possible and seeing to it that problems are not created at home.

Moreover, in her role as principal, Ms. Flowers is responsible for maintaining a balance among three criteria when determining a consequential course of action: professional norms and standards, community desires, and sound financial management.

John Banks would contend that there is no balance—that the criteria of professional norms and standards has been prostituted for community desires (in this case, the wish of one parent and the fear of the influence of that parent on other parents). Ms. Flowers, however, might contend that she is insuring the socialization of the young in a manner consistent with community norms and that John is alienated, to a degree, from those norms. Further, she has acted in a manner that she feels would cause the least amount of open conflict and will insure the harmony she desires.

What courses of action are open to Sara Flowers? She can take a stand in behalf of John's professional judgment and academic freedom. She can attempt to control him through cooptation or coercion. In the longer run she can scheme to get rid of him. But, in dealing with the immediate situation she does not have the time to establish a legitimate case for not renewing his contract. Does she have other alternatives?

Ms. Flowers is in a power advantage in all areas. John Banks is at a disadvantage. As has been noted, she is the superordinate in the school building hierarchy. She is not faced with the insecurity of a year-to-year contract. Her position within the formal hierarchy is supported with over twenty years of teaching in the local system. She, in all probability, has strong collegial ties across the system, as well as strong ties to and within all levels of the community at large. Additionally, her husband holds a prestigious position in the business sector and has ties with the state government. (The superintendent hopes to head in this direction.)

We are not told how professionally respected Ms. Flowers is among her peers and colleagues. We can only speculate that she has assumed her principalship through one of three means: seniority combined with loyalty and meeting certification requirements for a principalship; demonstrated administrative aptitude combined with acquiring principal certification; or she was certified as a principal and the school system needed to demonstrate compliance with an affirmative action plan. But, no matter how low her esteem, it seems safe to assume that Ms. Flowers still has a strong power base from which to operate.

It is advantageous also to consider how Ms. Flowers defines her function. To do this it is important to look at those things she emphasizes. From her demonstrated interest in the superintendent's campaign, her desire to maintain harmony, and her concern about problems the influential parent could cause, it seems appropriate to infer that she defines her function in terms of responsibilities to her superordinates and the community. An additional point to consider here is the fact that Ms. Flowers is the only female principal in the system. Consequently, she may feel a compelling pressure to prove herself to her superintendent, thereby further defining her function in terms of him. Little emphasis is given to maintaining a collegial tie to her teaching staff—at least not to John.

Because Ms. Flowers has taught in the local community most of her adult life and her husband is a successful local banker, she has been and always will be, relatively immobile as well as nonmobility oriented. Data exist that suggest that maintenance of the status quo is characteristic of less mobile administrators. Such administrators are often oriented to the values of the local community as opposed to their professional peers or a professional ideology. Ms. Flowers indicates that her "main concern is to maintain harmony"—certainly a concern for the status quo, but not necessarily an unconcern for progress. The religious and social values of the community are exceedingly important guides relative to her course of action in this situation. She is more oriented to the values of one (apparently strong) component of the community, than to a professional ideology.

AUTONOMY

The situation, as presented in the case study, deals largely with the concepts of academic freedom, authority and expertise. The conflict that arises is due in part to a threat to the amount of autonomy John Banks assumes is his.

Autonomy is an important factor to be considered in this situation. Autonomy is defined in terms of three implied elements: insulation (isolation), discretion, and interdependence. Apparently, John teaches in a self-contained classroom. Operating in this context removes him from a great deal of peer or administrator observation. Likewise, John is relatively isolated. If he received feedback from Ms. Flowers' one visit to his classroom during his first year, we are not aware of it. Further, John received only minimal advice from his peers during that time—and he probably solicited the advice he received.

From the data presented, it is probable that John is also relatively interdependent. Rather than relying on other school units in curricular matters, he appears to seek out resources from other agencies—like the Title III MRC.

Up to the point of conflict with Ms. Flowers, John either naively assumes that he operates in a context that allows for a wide range of alternatives relative to instructional matters or he is so preoccupied with endeavors such as his farm that he doesn't realize that he may actually have few alternatives. Possibly, the question has never been tested. John Banks assumes he possesses a great deal of autonomy.

Even though isolated in his classroom, John interacts with and teaches in front of a student audience. In reality, then, he works before a public that is composed of mutual runners—youngsters who carry home bits and pieces of what goes on in school. Parents sometimes react directly to those bits and pieces. This appears to be the case here.

John remains "autonomous" until Ms. Flowers receives the complaint. At that time teacher autonomy and administrator autonomy overlap. Soon thereafter, she visits his classroom twice in one week and eventually suggests that he delete all MACOS materials and topical considerations from his social studies lesson plans. In one fell swoop John's zone of autonomy, academic freedom, professional judgment, and idealism have been squarely challenged. Indeed, he is not as insulated or isolated as he has assumed. He does not possess the discretional latitude that he thought he possessed prior to being scrutinized by Ms. Flowers. Following that confrontation the alternatives are clearly fixed and understood. As was noted earlier, conflict can be predicted when principals act as official superordinates in instructional matters and fail to protect their staffs from outside constituencies.

ENVIRONMENT

At least two variables are important in an environmental analysis: the geographical region, and the specific community.

The fact that this situation occurs in the south and in a rural, and relatively small and fundamentalist community, is important. School systems are unique and differ significantly in their vulnerability to the publics they serve as well as to other clients that can easily penetrate their boundaries. They differ, then, according to the characteristics of the communities they serve.

Magnolia Elementary School is a community institution. As such it seeks to reflect the values of the community under the administration of Ms. Flowers, as well as Dr. Lazarus. Additionally, it is reasonable to assume that, collectively, the schools of Shelbyville provide a focus for the integration of community life. Overt pressures and demands from parents have a consequential impact, making the school a vulnerable organization, especially in this particular environmental context. But what about the possibility of the school having a shaping effect on the community—especially this community?

The institutionalization of school systems in small communities can be ascribed to three factors: the homogeneity of the community, the social and cultural integration of the school and immediate environment, and the degree to which local citizens are active in school affairs. Data to support the first two of the foregoing three factors are evident in the case study. We are not presented with data regarding the active interest of community members in the school. We can only speculate that it is more than minimal, given the degree of caution and concern evidenced by Ms. Flowers. John, however, does remark about the complaint lodged against him being based on second-hand information rather than direct observation or inquiry.

The fact that Shelbyville has apparently been voted dry on numerous occasions; that most of the teachers are graduates of an institution only 40 miles away; that the religious orientation of the community is fundamentalist; that most of the system's elementary teachers (and few of the total number of junior and senior high school teachers) do not participate in the Shelbyville Teachers Association; that the Association's small membership is considered liberal because it supports collective bargaining; that Shelbyville is located in a small, rural southern setting—all these considerations point to assessing Shelbyville as a homogeneous, conservative community. Its schools accurately mirror the community. Variables like autonomy, professional judgment, academic freedom, professional teaching norms and expertise are not a priority administrative concern—at least not at Magnolia Elementary School under the conditions at hand. In fact, such concerns may be meaningless to a large majority of the elementary teachers in the community; but not to John Banks—the untenured second year teacher.

COPING STRATEGIES

The outcome of the situation is yet to be determined. No more is known to the investigator at the time of this writing than has been presented. It appears, however, that John Banks does not intend to comply passively with Ms. Flowers' "suggestions." We do not know how militant he is, nor how militant he may become in the near future. But, from what we do know we can speculate, with some probable accuracy, that he will not comply; nor will he totally rebel. His ideal choice will probably be to work actively (but prudently) within the school system's organization to effect what he considers to be sound change. We do not know, however, if that will be an option available to him.

John's professional career in Shelbyville will, to a large degree, be dependent upon Dr. Lazarus—someone we know little about. We can conjecture that he is a logical extension of values of the community.

What if the problem confronts Dr. Lazarus prior to the election? How might he react? What if the problem is contained until after the election, Dr. Lazarus wins and the situation is passed to his successor? What kind of successor is Dr. Lazarus likely to recommend to the board? What kind of successor is the board likely to employ?

What if Dr. Lazarus loses the election? What if he loses due to the media picking up the local problem and sensationalizing it? If any of these "ifs" transpire, what will they mean to John Banks, to Sara Flowers, to the parent who initially complained or to parents of a similar persuasion? How vulnerable is the school organization relative to the environmental context? If the Shelbyville schools are community institutions, what potential do they have for shaping the community itself?

If John pushes his point and wins, will he or should he stay in Shelbyville? Does Ms. Flowers possess enough legitimate authority and a stong enough community power base to hinder John's long-term continuance in the school system?

What do you predict the outcome(s) to be? Why?

Activity 4

Writing a Case Study

Once participants have analyzed a case study or two, they might profit from writing case studies of their own. Writing case studies encourages participants to become more aware of and to apply concepts they have encountered elsewhere in the materials.

A case study tells a story of an event or related events and emphasizes one or more important concepts which the writer wishes to illustrate. The reader is led to analyze the events, to establish relationships among events and characters, and to propose his or her own ideas about what actions might influence or alter the case as it is written. In conjunction with this volume on schools, participants might develop a case around a school-related event which utilizes some of the following concepts:

1. Informal organization
2. Formal organization
3. Power
4. Authority
5. Responsibility
6. Prestige
7. Esteem
8. Competence
9. Status inconsistency
10. Emulation
11. Delegation
12. Slippage
13. Autonomy
14. Standardization
15. Direct supervision
16. Mutual adjustment
17. Scheduling
18. Reporting
19. Social environment
20. Coping strategies

The cases may be long or short; they may describe a single event or may become sequential cases where a series of events are described in parts as they unfold. A case might also be written as a letter to a friend explaining a situation in which the author finds himself or herself currently embroiled. Regardless of format, the case is likely to revolve around a conflict or potential conflict situation.

Some cases may be selected by the participants for group discussion. Others might be distributed and read independently. Whichever mode is chosen, the following questions are likely to apply:

1. Who are the case characters? What motivates their actions?
2. What organizations are involved in the case?
3. What problem or problems are illustrated?
4. What circumstances gave rise to the situation?
5. How might the situation have been handled by the characters?
6. What characteristics of organizations are illustrated in the case?

Additional questions will be raised and addressed during reading and group discussion.

Activity 5

Up the Down Staircase*

   Up the Down Staircase is a feature length film based on the best-seller book by Bel Kaufman which can be used to illustrate some of the major features of schools as organizations.

   It is suggested that before discussing the details of the film, all learners should consider its literary merits and limitations. The film does tend to exaggerate and stereotype. The plot is sketchy and sometimes moves slowly, and the characters are not well developed; for example, the central character, Miss Barrett, is never shown in any role other than the role of teacher.

   Nevertheless, the movie has some merits as an instructional device. It dramatizes the dilemmas that teachers and students face in some multiracial, big-city schools which are plagued with disorder. It demonstrates the social distance between teachers and parents, and between teachers and students. It underscores the incompatibility between bureaucracy and profession. It testifies to how professional standards can interfere with personal relationships. It shows how the particularistic values of parents clash with the universalism of teachers. And ultimately, the film is a tribute to some of the absurdities of bureaucracy in education.

   It is suggested that discussion questions should be raised before the participants view the film. Here are some suggestions:

- Take note of the types of organizations being portrayed. Identify the kinds of conflict portrayed by the various subcultures depicted in the film.

- Look for the characteristics of organizations that are in evidence in Calvin Coolidge High School. Consider whether these characteristics are also evident in your school and if they are manifested in the same ways, or differently.

- Observe the coping strategies Miss Barrett and other teachers use and consider their effectiveness.

- Consider how you might handle the situations in which Sylvia Barrett finds herself. Consider whether you would take the action she takes at the end of the film.

---

*   *This film can be rented through a Columbia Pictures distributor for approximately $50 per day. The book,* Up the Down Staircase *(Prentice-Hall, 1964) is published in paperback by Avon Books, a Division of the Hearst Corp., New York City. A list of other suggested films is contained in Volume I. See Appendix B. p. 81.*

MAJOR CONCEPTS

- Bureaucracy
- Hierarchy of Control
    Power
    Authority
    Direct Supervision
- Conformity
    Ritualistic Conformity
- Standardization (Order)
    Custodial Organization
    Goal Displacement
- Informal Organization
- Professional Employees
- Individual and the Organization
    Social Distance
    Impersonality
    Alienation
- Autonomy
    Discretion (freedom)

MAJOR FILM CHARACTERS

- Miss Sylvia Barrett—a first year teacher at Calvin Coolidge High School
- Mr. Paul Barringer—an English teacher and colleague of Miss Barrett
- Ferone—a delinquent student
- Bea Schachter—an experienced teacher and friend of Miss Barrett
- J.J. McCabe—administrative assistant at Calvin Coolidge High School

THE FILM IN BRIEF

This film depicts an insider's view of a large metropolitan high school and shows what happens as a dedicated new teacher's idealism begins to crumble in the face of a formidable bureaucracy, lack of communication, educational jargon and trivia.

As the film opens, Miss Sylvia Barrett approaches her first teaching assignment at Calvin Coolidge High School, a large barren school situated in a ghetto area of some large city. Upon entering the school, she is met by tumultuous confusion as a mass of anonymous students and teachers jostle one another in their rush through the crowded hallways. As she makes her way to her classroom an administrator passes and informs her abruptly that she is going up the wrong stairway.

The following scenes successively introduce administrators, clerks, a counselor, a nurse, and other characters, each of whom adds in one way or another to her frustration as she awakens to the engulfing stranglehold that the bureaucracy has on the educational process. In the classroom Miss Barrett learns how the students' apathy and their disdain for adult authority produces a constant fear of complete disorder. But through it all, she is coached by an experienced teacher, Bea, who gives her guidance and encouragement.

And yet, Miss Barrett also is learning something else: that beneath it all there is reason for some hope. As she challenges her students in class and learns to know them one by one, a few begin to reach out to her for attention and help.

The story unfolds in a series of dramatic incidents. There is the young student with a school girl crush on Mr. Barringer, a handsome but distant male teacher. She writes a love note to him. He responds only mechanically by correcting the grammar, returning it to her without comment on its substance. Finally frustrated by this teacher's apparent disinterest, the girl attempts suicide by jumping from his classroom window while he is away from school for an unauthorized reason.

In another encounter Miss Barrett's authority and her personal commitment are repeatedly tested by Ferone, a delinquent boy whom Miss Barrett tries to befriend without much success. When he finally pulls a knife on her, she is forced to report him to the administration, an act which will make her his permanent enemy.

Eventually Miss Barrett gives up and submits her resignation to the school authorities. But as the year wears on, she experiences some minor successes. For example, an alienated student becomes an active participant in a school play and reveals to her that he has been the anonymous author of several notes pleading for her attention and love.

As she ponders her first year, she decides that perhaps she can become an effective teacher after all, despite the obstacles. She withdraws her resignation as the film ends.

Up the Down Staircase — A Film Analysis

Ronald G. Corwin   Roy A. Edelfelt

The viewer of Up the Down Staircase is struck by the priority the school staff gives to order (standardization) and discipline (conformity).

This custodial function repeatedly intrudes on instruction and interferes with interpersonal relationships. There are the ever present rules about the window shades, library books, hall passes, locking desk drawers, and the abuse of staircases. Taking attendance, announcing complicated schedules, filling out forms, and related chores not only consume the staff's time but are considered to be at least as important as carrying on formal classroom instruction.

There is a hierarchy of control. The teachers watch the students, striving to maintain order in the classroom and hallways. The administration watches the teachers. The police hold the school officials responsible for the transgressions of students in the community. And the administration informs a teacher when "his" or "her" student has violated a rule. Several impersonal devices are employed to maintain order. The time clock is representative. Even parent-teacher conferences are regulated by arbitrary time limits, and more generally by a ceremonial evening set aside for this purpose. Even on this occasion, parents are welcomed by an unseen voice over the loudspeaker instructing them on procedures. Perhaps most striking, however, is the commanding authority of the bells. Teachers' commands are no match for the bells, which disrupt discussions mid sentence to signal the next activity. The students are thus moved through their day as if on a factory conveyor belt.

The preoccupation with order is starkly dramatized in the singular reaction of Mr. McCabe (the assistant principal) to the intellectual excitement generated in Miss Barrett's class: the class is too noisy. It is indeed ironic that Mr. Bester, the principal who visited the class, did not convey his favorable impressions to Miss Barrett until she forced the issue with her decision to resign. This was one of the few instances in which the supervision could have been personalized.

Indeed, even the crisis of life that occurred when a student attempted suicide provoked only bureaucratic responses: forms to be filled out by the teacher in charge, a reprimand to a teacher for evading the rules, and a librarian's anxiety about the student's overdue library books. None of the characters, including compassionate Miss Barrett, intended to visit the girl in the hospital or to console her parents.

The social distance between the school and its clients is portrayed in other ways as well. The teacher-parent conference, for example, centers on a universal issue that separates parents and teachers everywhere: the parent wants the child's extenuating circumstances to be taken into account. This would mean bending the rules, and Miss Barrett's training and her present circumstance dictate against such particularism. She is sympathetic, and one senses the bind she feels, but it is clear that she will treat this child no differently than other children. He will be measured against fixed standards, and judged a failure.

Note that the parents are expected to come to the teacher's territory, the school. There is no indication that the teachers would, or even could, visit parents in their homes, where they might be confronted with more knowledge than perhaps they want to have, or could use, about the personal circumstances of each child. This social distance between home and school comes into vivid focus in the taunts shouted at the frightened teachers as they trudge through the neighborhood to catch a bus to their own neighborhoods in remote parts of the city.

The film forcefully demonstrates the irrelevance of the school in the lives of many of the students. They are expected to appreciate English novels that are foreign to their circumstances, passively sit through classes, tests, and ceremonial assemblies, and attend school dances with the punch bowl and other symbols of middle-class decorum.

The corresponding disillusionment of the teachers is aptly drawn as well. Thus we see the satisfaction that an experienced teacher takes in her ability to get through her classes without incident and walk safely through the neighborhood streets to her bus. We see in Mr. Barringer an experienced, well-educated teacher who responds with mechanical impersonality and strained superiority when a child reaches out for affection. We see numerous instances of goal displacement: a school nurse who, prevented from treating wounds, is reduced to ritualistically serving tea to the children who come to her with injuries; a counselor—the one person in the system who is responsible for helping the students to work out their personal problems—whose sole response to bureaucracy has been to set up a filing system filled with glib jargon characterizing each child in a phrase or less.

The focus is Miss Barrett, fighting this overriding temptation to adapt mechanically to the rituals of the system. She is struggling to remember why she entered teaching. She sees the dehumanizing features of the school for what they are as she tries to reach an alienated and violent young man, Ferone. Accustomed to impersonal treatment from other teachers, he interprets her expression of professional concern as a personal, sexual overture. And, when he pulls a knife on her, she feels compelled to reassert her authority by reporting him, thus sacrificing a chance to negotiate with him on personal terms.

All of the control measures, the social distance, and the alienation, however, cannot destroy the fundamental autonomy of students and teachers in the system. Each group preserves its own subculture and identity. In the classroom this often translates into the loneliness of teaching—one teacher pitted against a class of students challenging that teacher's official authority at every opportunity. It also can mean ritualistic conformity and the opportunity to misuse freedom (discretion). And thus a student almost dies because a teacher was not in his classroom as he should have been. But it also means freedom to innovate in a class, to make the material meaningful to the students, and to convince them for one's expertise and concern. It means an occasional opportunity to overlook some rules, to let a student go to the bathroom without a hall monitor, and to defend him against false accusations. Outside of the classroom the private relationships among the teachers form the basis of an informal organization which provides some support against both the students and the administration. Thus, one teacher (Bea Schachter) warns another of a planned visit from the principal with the ominous signal "the ghost walks."

This last point highlights the pathos that runs through the film: The teachers are not using their informal strength to combat the oppressive bureaucracy. These professionally trained adults, coping with awesome responsibilities, are reduced to rueful pawns in an overbearing and aimless system. They are not uniting and striking out for improved conditions on behalf of the students, but instead are struggling to survive. And one by one, they have learned to survive by accepting, by conforming, by adapting. This leaves no one to push for reform, except an occasional idealistic newcomer, like Miss Barrett. But it is clear that, having given up the option of resigning Miss Barrett, too, must now learn to survive.

Postscript

In portraying teachers as often powerless individuals, sociologists, such as those represented in this volume, may startle many teachers who feel that they have taken substantial charge of their own professional destiny. But whether correct or not, sociological insights also might prompt teachers to see more clearly the possibilities of new modes of action to influence the rights and privileges of the teaching profession and to improve the school as a social system for students and teachers.

Teachers have had to work in situations where much is mandated, e.g., curriculum, personal and professional behavior, and conditions of work. Much of the effort to improve teaching, and ultimately to improve the quality of education has been external—instituting new curricula from without, legislating or decreeing higher standards for certification, mandating college credits for continuing licensing, and the like.

Were we still in an era prior to the 1940's reliance on this trickle-down approach might still be convincingly argued. But not today! Today's teachers are no longer prepared in a few years at a normal school. Almost all have completed at least four years of college. Liberal arts study and specialization in teaching fields are major parts of the preparation of all teachers, and they have spent an extended period of time student teaching in actual school situations. Many subscribe to professional role conceptions. They have become assertive in professional and political matters, and organized at local, state and national levels.

And yet, the people with authority in education—school administrators, leaders in higher education, state department officials—have been reluctant to have teachers take initiative and power. Perhaps partially as a result of this attitude, many teachers exhibit a loss of zeal and initiative during the course of their careers. Teachers are often restricted by the present school organization in their assignments to the narrow confines of the classroom. Organizational problems beyond the classroom, even though they may directly affect what happens in the classroom, are not perceived or understood. As a consequence, decisions are not influenced to any extent by teachers. For example, the group of students who constitute a particular class a teacher must teach may be selected by someone in authority without any consultation with the teacher, the students, or the parents. The collection of students who make up the class may be completely incompatible, making teaching almost an impossible task. The administrator may argue that there isn't time to involve teachers in scheduling students. Thus, an outside force makes decisions about both the grouping of students and how teachers spend their time— two decisions obviously counterproductive to good education for students. If teachers broaden the context of their concern and learn to understand and influence the larger context, there is the clear possibility that the organization of which they are a part can be altered to serve students better and to make teaching more satisfying. We hope teachers will consider themselves in several roles as they study and analyze the material presented, i.e., as employees of the school district, as members of teacher organizations, and as citizens of a community.

Our intent is to help teachers see themselves as members of organizations, and also to study organizations in a dispassionate way. The latter so that organizations, particularly the school, can be viewed objectively as an institution (a social system) that exists because of circumstances both deliberate and fortuitous.

We are convinced that the school as an organization must change if the learning of young people is to improve and personal circumstances of teachers are not apt to change much unless the social system of the school is changed. Individual teachers and teachers collectively will be better equipped to alter the social system/organization of school if they are aware of its dynamics, its norms, its power structure, etc. And if the organization cannot easily be changed, teachers who understand what they are a part of will be better prepared to cope with what exists or make intelligent decisions about when to get out. Even the last two alternatives change the system because of the changed attitudes one assumes if one stays, and/or the altered situation in the organization if one leaves.

The current organization of schools is not adequate either to provide quality education for students or to give teachers the kind of time, prerogative, and professional stimulation necessary for a vital profession. In this respect, schools are no different than many other social organizations. In fact, almost all organizations in our society are facing, or are being forced to face, the prospect of change as increasingly more people voice dissatisfaction with services and products, and demand a greater voice in decision making.

As in the first volume, our attention in this volume has revolved around schools as organizations. Yet, we have repeatedly seen that groups in the larger society, such as parents, government bodies and teacher organizations always must be taken into account. The third and final volume of this series, to be published soon, will concentrate on community, state and national forces that shape schools and classrooms.

Appendix

Instructional Mode, Goals, and Objectives *

INSTRUCTIONAL MODE

The instructional mode used during the Corps Member Training Institute was important in ensuring the effectiveness of the materials and the favorable responses of participants. Suggestions for the mode and tone of instruction follow:

1. *Instruction should occur in small groups.* Ideally participants should be organized in basic discussion groups of about 10 members with one instructor for each group. Diversity of background among group members with one instructor is highly desirable. Instructors should be flexible and vary the program to meet the demands of an evolving instructional process.

2. *Instruction should give attention to the needs and interests of participants.* The backgrounds and levels of sophistication of participants should be assessed prior to, or at the first meeting, so that planning and grouping is responsive to the diversity and needs of participants.

3. *Instructional expectations should be made public.* Participants should receive statements of training goals and objectives, how those goals and objectives will be achieved, and indicators of how the participants will be evaluated.

4. *Instruction should provide for intensive involvement of participants.* Special effort should be made to select case studies, papers, vignettes, readings, abstracts, and films that are particularly suited to participants who are preservice or inservice teachers. Small group discussion should be planned to give every participant an active part in establishing a rationale, making choices and decisions, and testing principles and theories inherent in different kinds of organizations.

5. *Instruction should capitalize on the temporary society created by the group itself.* Characteristics of the group, as illustrated in its governance and its social and work problems, may be used for analysis and diagnosis, providing a real situation with which individuals and groups can deal.

---

*Reprinted from volume one of this series by Corwin and Edelfelt, Perspectives on Organizations: Viewpoints for Teachers (Washington, D.C.: American Association of Colleges for Teacher Education, 1976), pp. 8-10.

6. *Instruction should deal with process problems and skills as part of instruction.* How and why people behave in certain ways in an organization is part of learning about organizations. As appropriate, participants should use illustrations of their own behavior to analyze why particular progress or achievement by a group has or has not been made.

7. *Instruction should engage participants directly with problems of analysis, diagnosis, and choice.* In part, this point reiterates numbers 4 and 5. In addition, participants should have instructors and speakers interpret and discuss field experiences, role-playing situations, and other experiences. In all of these activities, the purpose is to deal directly and personally with how effectively one can work through a problem in a logical, rational way.

8. *Instruction should provide a variety of activities.* Engaging the interest of people in studying organizations is not easy. A variety of activities enriches the training session; for example, case studies, film and vignette analysis, field-based study of various organizations, independent study, readings, and films which are appropriate for use in groups of various sizes.

9. *Instruction should include close guidance, monitoring, and evaluation of participants.* The instructor-participant ratio should allow some one-to-one contact, providing opportunities to discuss how the goals of the program fit those of the individual and to negotiate modifications when possible. Such modifications, of course, become a matter of record and provide some data for program evaluation. The instructor's responsibility for evaluation is continuous and should be done cooperatively with participants.

10. *Instruction should respect the status of all participants.* Although all participants (and instructors as well) are learners, each participant presumably has a different status based on his or her competence, experience, and power position. This is especially true if a group contains both preservice and inservice teachers. Each person's place in the hierarchy should be recognized and respected.

We recognize that these 10 points are appropriate to study in any field and all too often are unattainable for one or more reasons. Yet, a large part of the success of the Corps Member Training Institute was attributable to a continuous effort to follow these principles. Each person using this material for instructional purposes will need to decide how best to present the concepts based on ever-changing tradeoffs among the instructors' skills, the learners' needs, and the administrative support systems.

GOALS AND OBJECTIVES

The instructional setting described above and the materials contained in Parts II and III of this book work together, enabling participants to achieve certain goals and objectives. The goals and objectives are shared with participants so that everyone is aware of the purposes for studying organizations.

The overall goal of *Perspectives on Organizations* is to:

- Develop an awareness of the characteristics and functions of organizations, and of how organizations and individuals influence each other.

The program designed to help participants reach this goal includes instruction to:

- Enable participants to identify problems that result from or are aggravated by some characteristics of organizations.
- Provide participants with skills, enabling them to analyze organizations and organizational problems.
- Build participant interest in continuing independent study of organizations in the future.

When they have completed the program, participants should be able to demonstrate (through analysis and discussion of organizations) that they have:

- An understanding of why it is important to study organizations.
- A knowledge of some of the complexities resulting from membership in organizations.
- The ability to define organizations, social systems, bureaucracy, organization theory.
- An awareness of approaches used to study organizations.
- An awareness of some key features of organizations.
- An understanding of how the various functions of organizations are coordinated.
- An awareness of models that are useful for analyzing organizations.
- The ability to classify organizations according to typology.
- An understanding of how the social environment might affect the organization.
- A knowledge of strategies for coping in organizations.

These, and perhaps other objectives that participants will identify for themselves, should be achieved as a study proceeds. Participants and instructors will frequently want to refer back to these objectives to assess progress. The materials and activities designed to help achieve the objectives are contained in each book in this series.